Becoming God's Last Days Anointed Warrior

Workbook Series
Volume Three

Coming on a Cloud with Power & Great Glory

Lessons On

11. The Last Harvest - Followed by Destruction
12. Return of the King
13. The Kingdom of God Reigning on Earth
14. Great White Throne Judgment - New Heaven & New Earth
15. Christian Warriors - It's Time to Rise Up

A study guide in conjunction with
lectures and video lessons by

DR. DONALD BELL
MAJOR USMC RET.

Becoming God's Last Days Anointed Warrior
Workbook Series Volume Three: *Coming on a Cloud with Power & Great Glory*

March 2022
Copyright © Dr. Don Bell

All rights reserved. Printed in the United States of America. No part of this publication may be reproduced, stored in a retrieval system, or transmitted, in any form or by any means electronic, mechanical, photocopying, recording, or otherwise, without the prior written permission of the author.

Scripture taken from the Holy Bible, New International Version®, NIV®. Copyright © 1973, 1984, 201 Biblica, Inc.™ Used by permission of Zondervan. All rights reserved worldwide. www.zondervan.com The "NIV" and "New International Version" are trademarks registered in the United States Patent and Trademark Office by Biblica, Inc.™ All rights reserved.

Scripture quotations are from the Holy Bible, English Standard Version® (ESV®), copyright © 2001 by Crossway, a publishing ministry of Good Publishers. Used by permission. All rights reserved.

Scripture quotations taken from the New American Standard Bible®, Copyright © 1960, 1962, 1963, 1968, 1971, 1972, 1975, 1977, 1995 by Lockman Foundation, Used by permission. (www.lockman.org)

Because of the dynamic nature of the Internet, any web address or links contained in this book may have changed since publication and my no longer be valid. The views expressed in this work are solely those of the author and do not necessarily reflect the views of the publisher, and the publisher hereby disclaims any responsibility for them.

ISBN 978-1-943412-07-5

Published by -
Wilderness Voice Publishing, LLC
Canon City, Colorado USA
www.mcgmin.com

"A voice crying in the wilderness - proclaiming the good news of the coming Kingdom!"

Table of Content

Session Eleven: The Last Harvest —
         Followed by Destruction   4

Session Twelve: Return of the King   23

Session Thirteen: The Kingdom of God Reigning on Earth   50

Session Fourteen: Great White Throne Judgment —
         New Heaven & New Earth   74

Session Fifteen: Christian Warriors - It's Time to Rise Up   99

Ministry and Resource Information   133

THE LAST HARVEST

FOLLOWED BY DESTRUCTION

(Revelation 14 – 15; 16:1-9)

SESSION #11 – WORKBOOK
Intended For
"KINGDOM WARRIORS IN THE ARMY OF GOD"

Unveiling Mysteries in the "Book of Revelation"

Based upon the Book:
GOD'S ANOINTED WARRIORS
By
Dr. Donald Bell
Major USMC, Ret.

(Slides # 2 thru 4)

"BLESSINGS & WARNINGS"
SUMMARIZED IN SEVEN MAJOR EVENTS

The entire Book of Revelation is the prophetic unveiling of the Great War between the kingdom of God and the kingdom of the World for possession of the entire world of mankind. Over and over, we are presented with several important contrasts between light and darkness.

Between the devastations of the seven trumpets and the seven bowls of wrath yet to be poured out on the earth, there appears to be another series of "sevens."

These are seven victorious visions which briefly summarize the events during the final proclamation of the gospel of the Kingdom of God throughout the earth.

These blessings and warnings are culminated by the downfall of the kingdom of this world.

We will now examine a summarization of a series of seven events that take place from the time of the gathering of the Lord's 144,000 witnesses on Mt Zion until the launching of the first four Bowls of Wrath that will be poured out throughout the entire earth.

(Slides # 5 thru 8)

ONE: THE LAMB & HIS 144,000 TOGETHER ON MT. ZION
(Revelation 14:1-5)

In this section of Revelation, we are given spiritual eyes to see the Lamb of God standing on Mt. Zion together with His 144,000 disciples who are <u>the messengers of His light throughout the period of dark tribulations in the latter days.</u>

Simultaneously, the world is demanding that all professing Christians commit spiritual adultery and worship the Antichrist or they would be expelled from the earth.

> Certainly, a great number of professing believers listened to the demands from the world and turned from the Lord and:

> Therefore God gave them up in the lusts of their hearts to impurity, to the dishonoring of their bodies among themselves, because they exchanged the truth about God for a lie and worshiped and served the creature rather than the Creator, who is blessed forever! Amen. ***Romans 1:24-25***

However, the 144,000 who are standing with the Lord on Mt. Zion are the ones who maintain their spiritual virginity in the midst of great pressures and temptations.

> Their love for the Lamb of God who sacrificed His life for His people was of much greater value than their own lives.

> These are the warriors in the Kingdom of God who continue to hear the following voice of their Commander-in-Chief:

> "If anyone would come after me, let him deny himself and take up his cross and follow me. For whoever would save his life will lose it, but whoever loses his life for my sake and the gospel's will save it. <u>For what does it profit a man to gain the whole world and forfeit his life?</u> For what can a man give in return for his life? <u>For whoever is ashamed of me and of my words in this adulterous and sinful generation, of him will the Son of Man also be ashamed when he comes in the glory of his Father</u> with the holy angels." *Mark 8:34-38*

<u>Key Points:</u>

Now a little known truth that is not commonly taught is that there is a separate distinction among the saints in eternal life. All will be "perfectly" blessed, but all do not reach the same state of glory in the eternal kingdom. For example: Some will rule ten cities, some five, but most will be citizens. [1]

> God has prepared some of His people to do great things for Him on this earth; that is to fight the kingdom of darkness as mighty warriors.

> These are those in His army who, if they remain faithful to their calling, will have a leadership position in the eternal kingdom.

> Obviously, these will include the 144,000 "sealed Christian warriors" who will boldly proclaim the gospel of Christ with great signs and wonders in the midst of these end time events.

<u>**Consider this:**</u> **many may have been called to this leadership role, yet they did not forsake their lives and thus, did not achieve their full calling.**

> Many of us wrestle with this calling while living in the midst of our comforts. Those who have been called know it deep down inside of them; yet many are continually excusing their laziness by believing they will start tomorrow. However, tomorrow never seems to come.

> We need to fight these comfort-temptations that impede our calling to prioritize the Lord in our lives. Every one of us faces these temptations toward apathy as it is an ongoing attack from the enemy.

> We must continue to seek for our individual destinies that He is calling us to and preparing us for!

Notes:

_____
_____
_____
_____

---

[1] Luke 19:11-27

(Slides # 8 thru 11)

TWO: THE ANGEL & THE EVERLASTING GOSPEL
(Revelation 14:6-7)

> Then I saw another angel flying directly overhead, with an eternal gospel to proclaim to those who dwell on earth, to every nation and tribe and language and people. And he said with a loud voice, "Fear God and give him glory, <u>because the hour of his judgment has come</u>, and worship him who made heaven and earth, the sea and the springs of water." ***Revelation 14:6-7***

What is symbolized here is a final great evangelistic work of God's people proclaiming the Gospel of the Kingdom throughout the earth.

- ➤ This angelic vision symbolizes the truth that before the time of the end, the gospel message will be proclaimed to all peoples residing in every nation throughout the world.

- ➤ This is the mission of the 144,000 who have been anointed on Mount Zion and dispatched by their Commander-in-Chief into all the nations across the globe.

- ➤ This final gospel message will be a calling to mankind to repent and give glory to God, but <u>it will also contain the prophetic warning that final judgments are soon coming to the world.</u>

- ➤ Thus, this is the final proclamation of the gospel to the world. **<u>A last call to repentance!</u>**

All of mankind shall be well-acquainted with the gospel message of Jesus Christ before the final judgments fall on the earth.

- ➤ Many people will respond and be brought into everlasting life, but <u>the great majority of the world will blasphemy this message and persecutes those who proclaim it</u>.

- ➤ Those who scorn the message will be without excuse when they stand before the judgment seat of Almighty God.

Therefore, this vision of a gospel-proclaiming angel is symbolic of a short season of vigorous and rapid evangelism across the earth.

- ➤ An evangelistic mission that will go out in a power never before seen in the world; the power of Jesus Christ manifested in His body of the 144,000. **(John 14:12-14)**

Notes:
_____
_____
_____
_____

(Slides # 12 thru 15)

TWO: THE ANGEL & THE EVERLASTING GOSPEL

This final gospel proclamation will also occur in the midst of great tribulation when the Antichrist rises to power and is committed to wipe out the Kingdom of God from the face of the earth:

> He (the Antichrist) shall speak words against the Most High, and shall wear out (persecute) the saints of the Most High, and shall think to change the times and the law; and they shall be given into his hand for a time, times, and half a time (3 ½ years). *Daniel 7:25 (emphasize mine)*

Now what questions will be arising in the minds of many of His people during this time of tribulation?
- Why does God allow all of this?
- How long shall the glory of His name be trampled underfoot?
- How long shall the persecution of His people go unpunished?
- Thus, doubt will begin to creep into even the most faithful of God's people.

The times will be so dark and evil that it is probable that many of His people will believe that they are the only faithful ones who remain and depression will set in.
- But the Lord responds, *"Arise for you have a gospel to proclaim for there are yet 144,000 who have not bowed their knees to the Antichrist."*[2]

During the final proclamation of the eternal gospel, it may appear as if Christianity has all but disappeared from the earth. <u>You may feel alone, but He will never leave your side.</u>[3]

- In the world they will say, "Antichrist has made all things. Who is like unto the beast, and who can war with him?"

- But over against this claim, the people of the Lord cry out, "Fear God and give Him glory, for the hour of His judgment has come and worship Him who made heaven and earth…"

"For the hour of His judgment has come" indicates that this final message precedes the launching of the series of bowls of wrath which will shortly be poured out upon the earth.

Notes:
_____
_____
_____
_____

---
[2] 1 Kings 19 (modified for this scenario)
[3] Psalm 23:4

BREAK-TIME (Slides # 16 - 17)
(Slides # 18 - 19)

THREE: THE FALL OF BABYLON
(Revelation 14:8)

> Another angel, a second, followed, saying, "Fallen, fallen is Babylon the great, she who made all nations drink the wine of the passion of her sexual immorality." ***Revelation 14:8***

Now Babylon the great is a spiritual, idolatrous prostitute that makes nations drunk by the wine of her fornication.

- Being drunk with wine is a depiction of a helpless and shameful condition brought about by excessive drinking.

- Drunkards worship those Babylonian luxuries which provide physical and emotional pleasure as well as those people who encourage them in their drunken lifestyle.

- This drunkenness is manifested in one's love for materialism, entertainment, celebrity worship, adultery, pornography, homosexuality, obsession with worldly pleasures; these are the idols of the world. **These are drunk on the wine of Babylon**.

- Pop music industry in Babylon is dominated by drug-using rock stars who have become cult leaders for our youth. Their songs glorify rebellion against parents, drug abuse, immorality, violence, murder, and Satanism. Multitudes of American people know every lyric and sing along with every word. **These are drunk on the wine of Babylon**.

Babylon possesses that spirit of godlessness which continually lures the hearts of mankind away from their loving Creator.

- Her allurement is so powerful that she seduces hearts by the attractiveness of worldly delights which build **that great lie that "its all about me"** in their individual lives.

- Also, many who claim to be among God's people are enamored by the worldly beauty of this Babylonian whore and unknowingly, they are drawn away from the Lord by her alluring promises. **These also are drunk on the wine of Babylon**.

- There is no greater wrong done to our Lord than to prioritize the affections of our hearts upon the creation rather than the Creator who brought all things into existence.

Notes:
_____
_____

(Slides # 20 - 21)

THREE: THE FALL OF BABYLON

> Key Points:
>
> **By drinking her wine, the worshippers of Babylon shall receive the wrath of God as a burning fire within their souls.**
>
> ➢ This is a spiritual torment that is everlasting for never shall the worshippers of the beast ever again receive even one glimpse of God's love.
>
> ➢ Here upon the earth they received the things of the world, and God allowed His light to shine upon both the wicked and the good alike, but eternal agony awaits all those who choose to follow Satan and the Antichrist.
>
> ➢ These are "Babylonian patriots" who pledge their allegiance to this spiritual whore.

The final message proclaimed by the 144,000 messengers during the last days will most certainly include the call:

> ...."**Come out of her, my people**, lest you take part in her sins, lest you share in her plagues; for her sins are heaped high as heaven, and God has remembered her iniquities.
> *Revelation 18:4-5*

The Lord's call to come out of Babylon appears to be directed to those who have professed faith in Christ, yet continue to revel in the midst of the attractions of the world.

➢ Among these are also those religious minded folks and their feel-good, but false gospel which claims that a God of love would never relegate anybody to eternal destruction. **They are drunk on the wine of Babylon**.

> For this reason, her plagues will come in a single day, death and mourning and famine, and she will be burned up with fire; for mighty is the Lord God who has judged her." *Revelation 18:8*

This is the final warning to come out from her for she is about to be destroyed.
Come out now!

Notes:

(Slides # 22 - 23)

FOUR: WARNING AGAINST WORSHIPPING THE BEAST
(Revelation 14:9-11)

> And another angel, a third, followed them, saying with a loud voice, **"If anyone worships the beast and its image and receives a mark on his forehead or on his hand, he also will drink the wine of God's wrath, poured full strength into the cup of his anger, and he will be tormented with fire and sulfur in the presence of the holy angels and in the presence of the Lamb.** And the smoke of their torment goes up forever and ever, and they have no rest, day or night, these worshipers of the beast and its image, and **whoever receives the mark of its name**."
> *Revelation 14:9-11*

Among the strongest of emotions that will bind many into allegiance with the Antichrist is "patriotism."

➤ This is a blind and fanatical love for some earthly kingdom and its rulers.

➤ It has been a strong bond in powerful nations such as America, Russia, Nazi Germany, etc; countries in which allegiance was not forced but taught from their youth.

➤ The image of the beast will be worshipped with such a deep, strong passion very similar to those patriotic nations who have historically pledged allegiance to their rulers who they considered to be like gods.

The fearful punishment that awaits those who worship the beast is two-fold:

1. **They will drink the wine of the wrath of God.**
➤ The first judgment falls upon them while yet alive in this world and will be experienced when the seven bowls are poured out throughout the earth.

2. **They shall suffer the fiery punishment of hell.**
➤ The second occurs in the world to come - warning that there is a much worse fate for taking the mark; **for the punishment of those who accept the "mark of the beast" is eternal.**

Our Lord, in His merciful and long-suffering love for mankind, patiently warns people concerning the consequences of rendering allegiance to Antichrist.

➤ This warning is not a threat, but is His last call from our Lord to leave Babylon and embrace His eternal love.

➤ This will also be a message proclaimed by the 144,000 end-time messengers during their last 3 ½ year ministry. **"Do not take the Mark of the Beast!"**

(Slides # 24 thru 26)

FIVE: BLESSED ARE THOSE WHO DIE IN THE LORD FROM NOW ON
(Revelation 14:12-13)

> **Here is a call for the endurance of the saints, those who keep the commandments of God and their faith in Jesus.** And I heard a voice from heaven saying, "Write this**: Blessed are the dead who die in the Lord from now on."** "Blessed indeed," says the Spirit, "that they may rest from their labors, for their deeds follow them!" *Revelation 14:12-13*

"Here is a call for endurance of the saints" is evidently a warning that is expressed in the strongest of terms.

Remember the Lord's instruction given to His people during the reign of Antichrist:

> If anyone is to be taken captive, to captivity he goes; if anyone is to be slain with the sword, with the sword must he be slain. **Here is a call for the endurance and faith of the saints**. *Revelation 13:10*

> **This call for endurance tells us that in the midst of persecution and suffering that His people are to remain calm and submissive.**
> ➤ They do not try to gain control of things by force. Even though they cannot buy nor sell, they do not use weapons to obtain what they want.
>
> **Their suffering will not persuade them to deny their God.**
> ➤ Even though the smallest of compromise might gain them favor and keep them out of prison and feed them, they will refuse to compromise.
>
> **How will they be encouraged to bear this suffering?**
> ➤ They know their captors will not escape from eternal destruction and that they themselves will receive an eternal crown of glory for their steadfast righteousness.

➤ **For they trust and embrace these words from the Lord:**

> And I heard a voice from heaven saying, "Write this: Blessed are the dead who die in the Lord from now on." "Blessed indeed," says the Spirit, "that they may rest from their labors, for their deeds follow them!" *Revelation 14:13*

The word is clear; faithfulness to Christ may result in martyrdom, but those who persevere are the true victors in the battle between the two kingdoms.

Notes:

_____

_____

BREAK-TIME (Slides # 27 - 28)

(Slides # 29 thru 31)

SIX: THE HARVEST OF THE EARTH
(Revelation 14:14-16)

> *The Harvest of the Earth*
> Then I looked, and behold, a white cloud, and seated on the cloud one like a son of man, with a golden crown on his head, and a sharp sickle in his hand. And another angel came out of the temple, calling with a loud voice to him who sat on the cloud, **"Put in your sickle, and reap, for the hour to reap has come, for the harvest of the earth is fully ripe**." So he who sat on the cloud swung his sickle across the earth, and the earth was reaped. ***Revelation 14:14-16***

The harvest will definitely be gathered but not until it is fully ripe and only God the Father knows this hour.

- Here we see an angel who comes out from before the presence of the Father and announces to the Son of God that the reaping may begin. This means that everyone who will come into the eternal Kingdom of God has now come in.

The actual reapers are the angels. This is the fulfillment of:

> And he will send out his angels with a loud trumpet call, and they will gather his elect from the four winds, from one end of heaven to the other. ***Matthew 24:31***

Jesus also spoke of this time when He said:

> Then two men will be in the field; one will be taken and one left. Two women will be grinding at the mill; one will be taken and one left. Therefore, stay awake, for you do not know on what day your Lord is coming. ***Matthew 24:40-42***

> **It appears that God's people who are alive during this time are now being separated from those places where the wrath of God is about to be poured out on the earth.**
>
> - This is the time when the "good seeds" who are God's people in the midst of the world will be separated from the "weeds" that Satan had sown among the "good seed."[4]
>
> - When the people of God have been separated to places of safety, then the destruction of the wicked symbolized by the harvest of the grapes, may proceed.
>
> - Thus, it appears that there will be a short period of time during which there are no more Christians living in the midst of the world but have been separated into their respective wilderness place.

---
[4] Matthew 13:24-30

> These are those who have been set apart until they behold the coming of the King of kings.

(Slides # 32 thru 34)
SEVEN: GOD'S WRATH FALLING UPON THE WORLD OF EVIL
(Revelation 14:17-20)

Then another angel came out of the temple in heaven, and he too had a sharp sickle. And another angel came out from the altar, the angel who has authority over the fire, and he called with a loud voice to the one who had the sharp sickle, "Put in your sickle and gather the clusters from the vine of the earth, for its grapes are ripe." <u>So the angel swung his sickle across the earth and gathered the grape harvest of the earth and threw it into the great winepress of the wrath of God. And the winepress was trodden outside the city, and blood flowed from the winepress, as high as a horse's bridle, for 1,600 stadia (about 184 miles).</u> *Revelation 14:17-20*

Here we see an angel coming out from the presence of the altar which lies before the throne of God.

> Underneath this altar is where the martyrs of Christ have been calling out for vengeance against the enemies of the Lord.

> But the Lord told them to wait until all of their fellow servants who were yet to be martyred are complete. [5]

For history must first run its course:

> The gospel must first be preached to all nations to allow all of mankind the opportunity to repent and turn to the Lord.

> The kingdom of the Antichrist must be fully manifested where there is no gray area between good and evil. Every soul will visibly stand either for Christ or for Antichrist.

> The wickedness of the earth must be full, and the remnant of the Lord separated apart from the worshippers of the Beast.

When that time arrives, the vengeance of Almighty God will fall upon all of the dark nations of the earth.

> Here the governing forces of this dark world will be trodden down in His winepress resulting in the squashing of millions and millions of those who embraced the Antichrist as their messiah.

> These are the great and mighty kings of the world who have gathered together with all of their loyal followers for the purpose of wiping out all of the Lord's beloved people from the face of the earth once and for all.

> The smashing of these kings and their armies will be so great that their blood will run four feet deep over a course of approximately 184 miles.

It will begin with the pouring out of the first five bowls of wrath resulting in tremendous devastation and suffering throughout the earth.

---
[5] Revelation 6:10-11

> Suffering that will not bring repentance, but will visibly reveal the evil hearts of mankind as they continue to blasphemy the Lord.

Then with the 6th bowl, we witness a gathering together of all the kings of the earth and their dark armies at Armageddon which, unknown to them, is really the winepress of God's wrath which will be manifested with the pouring out of the 7th bowl.

> The next session provides a descriptive scenario of this last great battle.

These seven bowls called the "wrath of God" are His holiness falling upon the world of sin.

> God's kingdom people made great and wonderful changes within this world throughout history, and millions came into the Kingdom of God. However, the dark evilness of the world has also continued to grow stronger and stronger.

> Now God the Father and His Son will release their holiness from heaven against this darkness which will utterly destroy this world of sin.

First, comes great worldwide destruction, but it will soon be followed by a great cleansing which will restore the earth to the days of the Garden of Eden.

Notes:

(Slides # 35 - 36)

HEAVEN CELEBRATES WHILE THE WORLD BLASPHEMIES
(REVELATION 15)

<u>Key Points:</u>

In Revelation 15, we see a victorious army of those martyred for their testimony now standing in heaven on a sea of glass mingled with fire.

➢ During their lifetime on earth, they passed through fiery trials from the enemy until the time came for their martyrdom.

➢ Now they stand in victory amidst the fires of heaven which, like Nebuchadnezzar's fiery furnace, will not harm the children of God, but will totally destroy His enemies.[6]

Among this victorious army are those who refused to worship the Antichrist even though they could neither buy nor sell nor live in the midst of that society.

➢ They were outcasts, many imprisoned and tortured, many betrayed by friends and loved ones, many terribly executed for their faith.

➢ They were tested to the extreme yet they continued to call upon the Lord for their strength.

➢ They fought the fiercest of all battles, and they were continuously sustained by their faith in the Lord Jesus whom they knew would one day come as the victorious King of kings.

➢ Now they stand alongside this sea of glass mingled with fire and singing the song of great victory before the Throne of God.

➢ Yes, this is a time of special privilege for the army of God who fought the greatest and most challenging of all battles. They stood up against Satan and his king, the Antichrist during the greatest tribulation this world had ever known.

These are those who received the following words of Jesus with an uncompromising heart:

"Blessed are you when others revile you and persecute you and utter all kinds of evil against you falsely on my account. Rejoice and be glad, for your reward is great in heaven, for so they persecuted the prophets who were before you. *Matthew 5:11-12*

---

[6] Daniel 3:8-30

(Slides # 37 - 38)

HEAVEN CELEBRATES WHILE THE WORLD BLASPHEMIES
(REVELATION 15)

> **But, is this multitude standing alongside the fiery sea of glass limited only to those warriors who fought during the Great Tribulation? <u>Certainly not!</u>**
>
> ➤ Warriors of God have fought this same battle throughout all the ages even though it rages most severely during this era of the end-times antichristian kingdom.
>
> ➤ Abraham fought this battle. Moses fought this battle. David fought this battle.
>
> ➤ All the witnesses and prophets of the Old Testament era fought this same battle.
>
> ➤ All the witnesses and martyrs of the New Testament era also fought this same battle.
>
> **Therefore, it is certainly true that all who have remained faithful from Abel to the very last witness in the Kingdom of God on earth shall stand by the fiery sea of glass singing their <u>song of Moses and of the Lamb</u>.**

> **The combining of these two songs embrace both the Old Testament and New Testament eras as one kingdom. Old and new dispensations shall be one; there is no break, no difference between them in glory.**
>
> ➤ This scene of mighty warriors who had conquered the beast and its image should remind us of the children of Israel standing on the edge of the Red Sea looking back over those waters that had just consumed their Egyptian enemies.
>
> ➤ The greatest and most powerful army in the world of that age had just been completely annihilated because they were attempting to slaughter a nation that God had raised up to manifest His glory throughout the world.
>
> ➤ At this point Moses and the Israelite people began to sing the "song of Moses" unto the Lord glorifying Him and giving thanks for this miraculous deliverance from their enemies.[7]
>
> ➤ The heavenly "sea of glass" is a reminder of the Red Sea which delivered the Israelites and destroyed their enemies; it is also a reminder of the great flood which delivered Noah and his family and destroyed the enemies of God.

---

[7] Exodus 15:1-18

> These were waters whereby the Lord provided both salvation for His people followed by destruction of their enemies.

BREAK-TIME (Slides # 39 - 40)
(Slides # 41 - 42)

THE FINAL JUDGMENTS OF OUR LORD BEGIN
(REVELATION 16:1-9)

The Seven Bowls of God's Wrath

> Then I heard a loud voice from the temple telling the seven angels, "Go and pour out on the earth the seven bowls of the wrath of God." *Revelation 16:1*

> **This final series of plagues that will be poured out upon all of mankind parallels the trumpet judgments that previously tormented the inhabitants of the earth.**
>
> ➢ Now the trumpet judgments affected only one-third of the earth yet provided an opportunity for millions to awaken and embrace the Lord through the testimony of the witnesses of Jesus Christ.
>
> ➢ However, these seven bowl judgments will devastate a world at a time when the testimony of Christ has been silenced.

This is the time of the final battle in a war that has raged since the fall of mankind in Eden.

➢ **It is the time** when the martyrs under the altar in the heavenly temple were waiting for:

> They cried out with a loud voice, "O Sovereign Lord, holy and true, how long before you will judge and avenge our blood on those who dwell on the earth?" *Revelation 6:10*

➢ **It is the time** when our Sovereign Lord fulfills His promise when He answered them:

> ………..rest a little longer until the number of their fellow servants and their brothers should be complete, who were to be killed as they themselves had been. *Revelation 6:11*

➢ **It is the time** for the righteous judgment of God to be poured out across the earth:

> …since indeed God considers it just to repay with affliction those who afflict you, *2 Thes. 1:6*

Notes:
_____
_____
_____
_____
_____

(Slide # 43)

1st Bowl Of God's Wrath Poured Out ------ On The Earth:

Harmful and painful sores break out upon everybody who bore the "mark of the beast."

➢ This will be very nasty as Job, a servant of God, can testify. Recall that Satan attacked Job, the beloved of God, with boils throughout his body.[8]

➢ Now Satan's worshippers are suffering a similar fate, but without any hope of being healed. Perhaps these sores will be seen as a worldwide plague.

➢ Certainly these suffering people will be crying out to their god, the Antichrist, for miraculous healing. **But, it won't happen!**

Notes:
_____
_____
_____
_____

(Slide # 44)

2nd Bowl Of God's Wrath Poured Out ------ On The Seas:

All the oceans around the world become like the "blood of a corpse."

➢ Now there can be no question in the minds of all the inhabitants of the earth that this is more than just a passing plague. God is raining judgment down upon the earth.

➢ Again, they will turn to their Antichrist and call upon him to heal the seas with his miraculous power. **But, it won't happen!**

Notes:
_____
_____
_____
_____

---

[8] Job 2:7-8

(Slide # 45)

3rd Bowl Of God's Wrath Poured Out ------ On Rivers & Springs:

All the fresh waters from streams, lakes, and rivers across the earth turn into blood.

Listen to the response from God's angel who was placed in charge of the waters on the earth:

> ..... they have shed the blood of saints and prophets, and you have given them blood to drink. It is what they deserve!" *Revelation 16:6*

These bowls of wrath poured out upon the earth are not about vengeance. The judgments of God are not vengeful. They are an expression of His righteous nature and His intense hatred of sin.

Listen to the response to these judgments from out of the altar where the souls of the martyrs reside and also where the prayers of the saints rise up before the throne of our Almighty God:

> And I heard the altar saying, "Yes, Lord God the Almighty, true and just are your judgments!" *Revelation 16:7*

> **Contrary to this viewpoint within the Kingdom of God, imagine the fear and confusion in the Kingdom of the World as suffering and frightened people cry out:**
>
> ➢ "Antichrist, our god, where are you? Remember your promises. Don't you care? Please, help us." **But, it won't happen!**

(Slide # 46)

4th Bowl Of God's Wrath Poured Out ------- On The Sun:

> Here the wrath of God is poured out upon the sun resulting in tremendous scorching heat falling upon a populace that is covered with painful boils and having only bloody waters to drink.
>
> ➢ Yet, even in their unimaginable suffering, they will continue to curse Almighty God and look to their Antichrist for their deliverance from God's wrath:
>
> "O' our beloved antichrist, please stop this. We've suffered enough. Remember your promises to take care of us." **But, it won't happen!**

Notes:
_____
_____
_____
_____
_____
_____

THE NEXT SESSION:

First Read: Revelation 16:10 – 21 plus 19:11 – 21)

THE RETURN OF THE "KING"

- The Last Three Bowls of God's Wrath are Poured Out
- A Detailed Overview of the Battle of Armageddon
- Satan's Final Mission Strategies
- The Glorious Descent of the Messiah to the Mt. of Olives
- The 2nd Coming of Jesus Christ as the "King of kings"
- The "Lake of Fire" Receives its First Victims

THE LAMB OF GOD - OUR TRUE "COMMANDER-IN-CHIEF"

The days are rapidly approaching when a tremendous separation will take place among mankind.

Yet, during this present era of warfare, He reigns as our Commander-in-Chief and His Name continues to be the battle cry for those warriors who fight daily for righteousness and truth.

His name is Jesus, Our Lord, Our King, Our Commander-in-Chief

- A truly mighty Leader who would never delegate assignments to His people that He Himself wouldn't readily embrace.

- A Commander that Christian warriors will readily follow not matter the danger or what costs have to be paid.

- These are warriors whose deepest desire is to hear Jesus welcome them with the following words when they enter into His presence:

.... 'Well done, good and faithful servant. You have been faithful over a little; I will set you over much. Enter into the joy of your master.' *Matthew 25:21*

THE RETURN OF THE KING

(Revelation 16:10-21; 19:11-21)

SESSION #12 – WORKBOOK
Intended For
"KINGDOM WARRIORS IN THE ARMY OF GOD"

Unveiling Mysteries in the "Book of Revelation"

Based upon the Book:
GOD'S ANOINTED WARRIORS
By
Dr. Donald Bell
Major USMC, Ret.

(Slides # 2 thru 5)

THE STATE OF THE WORLD AT THE POURING OUT OF "THE SEVEN BOWLS OF GOD'S WRATH"

All the civilized nations of the world have enthroned the Antichrist as their hope for eternal security and happiness. They admire him, they worship him, and they bow down and acknowledge him as the greatest of all kings.

- Now they can live life any way they want as long as they continue to worship the image of the Beast. Sorcery, idolatry, pornography, adultery, homosexuality, same-sex marriage, abortion, child sacrificing, pedophile acts, etc. will all be acceptable and commonplace.

- Everything that despises and opposes the commandments of our Lord will be embraced. Antichrist is their messiah as well as their hope for eternal salvation.

The small surviving remnants throughout the earth that refuse to obey him have all become social outcasts and are probably in hiding while being provided for by the Lord.[9]

- These will be end-times prayer warriors who are passionately calling for of the return of their King, Jesus Christ.
- It is at this point in time that God the Father will visibly demonstrate His all-powerful sovereignty.
- It is a time for the pouring out of the seven bowls of God's wrath throughout the earth.

Notes:

---

[9] Psalm 23:5

(Slides # 6 - 7)

AN OVERVIEW OF THE FIRST FOUR BOWLS OF WRATH

Our Lord will decree through the first "four bowl judgments" that:

➢ All those who worship the Beast will not be able to buy nor sell, for He is taking it all away from them.

➢ The crops, the rain, the food, the water, the medicines, the wealth of the earth; it all disappears.

<u>FIRST</u> - harmful and painful sores & boils - breaking out upon everybody - who bore the "mark of the beast."

<u>SECOND</u> - all the oceans around the world become like the "blood of a corpse."

<u>THIRD</u> - All the fresh waters from streams, lakes, and rivers across the earth turn into blood.

<u>FOURTH</u> - The wrath of God is poured out upon the sun resulting in tremendous scorching heat falling upon a populace that is covered with painful boils - and having only bloody waters to drink.

Just as Antichrist had done to God's people, so now God does to the people of Antichrist.

➢ Yet, as the first four bowls of wrath are poured out, the world will continue their hateful blasphemies of God. Antichrist continues to be their hope for deliverance.

At this point, it is time to demonstrate the impotence of Antichrist before the world.

Notes:
_____
_____
_____
_____
_____
_____
_____
_____
_____

(Slides # 8 - 10)

5ᵀᴴ BOWL OF GOD'S WRATH
"POURED OUT ON THE THRONE OF THE BEAST"

> The fifth angel poured out his bowl on the throne of the beast, and its kingdom was plunged into darkness. People gnawed their tongues in anguish and cursed the God of heaven for their pain and sores. <u>They did not repent of their deeds.</u> ***Revelation 16:10-11***

Key Points:

When the 5ᵗʰ bowl is poured out, a great darkness descends over the Antichrist's throne and spreads throughout his entire kingdom.

- ➤ All of his followers begin to gnaw their tongues in anguish. It is difficult to imagine the effect of this darkness; but it will certainly intensify the distress of the previous four plagues.

- ➤ Following on the heels of a "**scorching sun**" <u>this darkness will probably cause a tremendous "**freezing**" across his kingdom.</u>

- ➤ Yet, even in the extreme distress which has been launched upon the world of mankind, these people will continue to blasphemy Almighty God.

- ➤ The Holy Spirit who draws mankind unto the Lord is no longer available to those who have taken the "mark of the beast."

- ➤ Their anger demonstrates that they do not doubt the existence of God, but their hard and rebellious hearts hate Him more and more as bowls of wrath continue to fall upon the earth.

- ➤ Up to this point, the people of Antichrist have dedicated both their earthly and eternal lives into his care; but now, as they see their worldly messiah's throne covered in darkness, they will most likely begin to doubt his divine power and authority.

These are the same people who had previously declared:

> ...."Who is like the beast, and who can fight against it?" ***Revelation 13:4***

➤ **Jesus Christ, our true Commander-in-Chief says, "I can!"**

Notes:
_____
_____
_____
_____

(Slide # 11)

6TH BOWL OF GOD'S WRATH
"POURED OUT ON THE EUPHRATES RIVER"

During this period of painful darkness which has obliterated the glory of Antichrist in the world, the intensity of hatred toward our Lord has reached a boiling point unlike any period in the history of the world.

The land of Israel, where the kingdom of God was physically established four thousand years ago, has been chosen to be the location of the final battle between the kingdom of God and the dark armies of Satan's kingdom.

<u>The first "6th bowl event"</u> to take place is the "drying up of the Euphrates River."

> The sixth angel poured out his bowl on the great river Euphrates, and its water was dried up, to prepare the way for the <u>kings from the east.</u> *Revelation 16:12*

<u>Key Points:</u>

➢ The Euphrates River has always been the eastern boundary line between Israel and the heathen nations.

➢ From a spiritual sense, the Euphrates River is symbolic of the boundary line between God's people and their enemies.[10]

So why is the drying up of this river so important during this period of time?

➢ It is a spiritual invitation from the Lord calling all the heathen armies to a battlefield located in the land where He has historically manifested His power and glory to both His people and their enemies.

The "kings from the east" appear to be representative of pagan populations in the eastern oriental regions. They probably include the following nations that have the greatest populations; China, Japan, India, Indonesia, Pakistan, Afghanistan, Iran, Iraq etc.

➢ These comprise the worshippers of the gods of Buddhism, Hinduism, and Islam who have persecuted the Christians in the midst of their countries for centuries.

➢ Their armies will surely include millions of foot soldiers who will march across the dried-up riverbed of the Euphrates.

Notes:

_____

_____

---

[10] Hoeksema, Herman, *Behold, He Cometh,* (Grand Rapids: Reformed Free Publishing Assn, 1969) p.546

(Slides # 12 thru 14)

6ᵀᴴ BOWL OF GOD'S WRATH
"THREE UNCLEAN FROG-LIKE SPIRITS ARE RELEASED"

The second "6th bowl event" that arouses the armies around the world to align against the Kingdom of God are unclean spirits which proceed out of the mouths of the unholy trinity; that being, Satan, Antichrist, and the False Prophet.

> And I saw, coming out of the mouth of the dragon and out of the mouth of the beast and out of the mouth of the false prophet, three unclean spirits like frogs. For they are demonic spirits, performing signs, who go abroad to the kings of the whole world, to assemble them for battle on the great day of God the Almighty. *Revelation 16:13-14*

➢ This is a powerful spiritual force that will infect millions and millions of kings, religious leaders, generals and their armed soldiers worldwide with a demonic spirit --- a spirit that will replace any semblance of morality with a deep hatred to rape and murder all those who live in the nation of Israel.

> And they assembled them at the place that in Hebrew is called **Armageddon**. (Rev. 16:16)

The kings from the east will organize and unite with the forces of Antichrist from the Western and Middle Eastern countries on the plains of Megiddo, commonly referred to as Armageddon.

Now Armageddon is merely the gathering place for the world's armies; not the site of the last great battle.

➢ The real battle will take place in the Valley of Jehoshaphat, otherwise known as the Kidron Valley that lies between the temple mount in Jerusalem and the Mount of Olives. **(Joel 3:1-2)**

This demonically possessed army will number in the millions and it would certainly appear to the natural eye that the nation of Israel will be quickly and completely destroyed.

➢ Yet, our Commander-in-Chief again alerts His people residing in Israel to remain vigilant and not be fearful or deceived by this tremendous darkness that appears to be unstoppable in its mission to finally annihilate the Kingdom of God.

➢ For this is the final event that precedes the second coming of Jesus Christ, the promised Messiah and the Son of God.

> "Behold, I am coming like a thief! Blessed is the one who stays awake, keeping his garments on, that he may not go about naked and be seen exposed!" *Revelation 16:15*

BREAK-TIME *(Slides # 15 - 16)*

(Slides # 17 thru 19)

SATAN'S HISTORIC MISSION STRATEGIES – AN OVERVIEW

> **The historic tactic used to accomplish Satan's purposes has always been "<u>deception</u>."**
>
> ➢ He has deceived mankind into believing that the potential that resides within each of us can be more fully realized by living life under our own guidance rather than under God's.
>
> ➢ However, in order to truly experience the worldly self-life style, Satan must remove all those who are not deceived and are totally committed to almighty God and to His Son, Jesus Christ.
>
> ➢ Satan has historically done this by convincing world governments, together with false religions, that God's people are the only obstacle that keeps them from achieving their worldly goals, and so they must be either converted to the world's belief system or killed.
>
> ➢ If he could prevent all of mankind from reflecting God's glory upon the earth, then Satan himself would be the recipient of worship and glory throughout the earth.
>
> ➢ Thus, he could claim that he is now in control of all those initially created in the "image of God," for they have been reborn into the "image of Satan."

However, Satan also knows that his time is short for he too recognizes the signs that precede the return of Jesus Christ and His mighty army.

➢ This is no secret; Satan understands what is shortly ahead and he needs to defeat the purposes of God for His Son in order to set his throne above that of God and to avoid his eternal destruction.[11]

➢ He knows that he needs to prevent this return of Christ or He must overwhelm and defeat Him with an earthly and demonic army prepared to engage Him when He sets foot on the Mount of Olives.

Notes:

---

[11] Isaiah 14:12-21; Ezekiel 28:13-19

(Slides # 20 thru 23)

SATAN'S NEW STRATEGY
FRONTAL ATTACK ON THE LAND OF ISRAEL

The time for these tactics of "deception" has passed. It is now time for a frontal assault on the beloved land of Israel and its inhabitants who have refused to render allegiance to the Antichrist.

➢ This was the "Promised Land" created by our Lord to manifest His glory throughout the world, and now it has been chosen to be the final battlefield between the spiritual forces of God and Satan, as well as the physical forces of Jesus Christ and the Antichrist.

This unholy trinity obviously believes that they are the ones initiating this final war against the Kingdom of God.

➢ However, it is really our Lord who, in His timing, has planned this gathering together of His enemies from out of every tribe and nation:

> I will gather all the nations and bring them down to the Valley of Jehoshaphat. **(This is the Kidron valley which lies between the Mount of Olives and the City of Jerusalem).**
> And I will enter into judgment with them there, on behalf of my people and my heritage Israel, because they have scattered them among the nations and have divided up my land, and have cast lots for my people, and have traded a boy for a prostitute, and have sold a girl for wine and have drunk it. *Joel 3:2-3 (emphasis mine)*

The time has now come:

➢ For a frontal assault on the land of Israel and those inhabitants who have refused to render allegiance to the Antichrist.

➢ To manifest the power and the glory of God our Father and His Son, Jesus Christ unto all the nations of the world.

➢ To bring about both an external and spiritual cleansing to the land of Israel by purging the nation of its secular idolatry.

➢ To remove the powers of darkness from within the nations across the earth and bring them into the valley of God's judgment where they will be violently destroyed. <u>Those people who remain in all the nations will then have the opportunity to receive and worship the Lord during the coming millennial reign of Jesus Christ.</u>[12]

➢ This is the second coming of the Son of God; only this time He comes as the Lion of Judah for He will bring sudden and total destruction to the enemies of His people

➢ Then He will establish His physical reign as the King of kings over the nations of the earth.

Notes:

---
[12] Zechariah 14:16; Isaiah 52:10; 66:20; Psalm 86:9

(Slides # 24 thru 26)

MASSIVE DEMONIC ARMIES GATHER AT ARMAGEDDON
Revelation 16:16

Remember that Armageddon is merely the gathering place for the world's armies; not the site of the last great battle.

- The real battle will take place in the Valley of Jehoshaphat, otherwise known as the Kidron Valley that lies between the temple mount in Jerusalem and the Mount of Olives.

Now comes the launching of the final great battle of this age between the evil kingdom of the world and the holy kingdom of God - a confrontation that has been building for six thousand years. **Note:**

> Very little detail concerning this final battle is provided in the Book of Revelation. However, some of the Old Testament prophets, especially <u>Zechariah and Joel</u>, provide additional insights which assist in picturing this end-time event.

<u>A Description of these Demonic Armies:</u>

Satan has gathered together his legions of "Human-Orcs" with the ultimate mission of defeating the purposes of our Lord for mankind. A victory in this final battle would allow him to grab the reins of control over the entire world.

- For those who have seen the movie, "The Lord of the Rings" you will recall the deep evil that is manifested in the terrible appearance of the "Orcs" which comprise the army of a dark lord in the movie.

- The term "Human-Orcs" is meant to convey a picture of the inner hearts of these end-times forces that will run to the war when called forth by the demons of Satan, Antichrist, and the false prophet.

- They have a visible murderous and gnawing hatred for those who oppose the reign of their evil god over the entire earth. They growl, slobber, and gnaw their teeth while awaiting orders to launch a murderous attack on the nation of Israel.

- These massive, demonically empowered armies are representative of the hatred that has expressed itself throughout human history in hostility toward, and persecution of, the people of God.

Now when these massive armies have gathered at Armageddon, they will coordinate their plans for conquering the land and eliminating the nation of Israel from the face of the earth.

When these demonic armies launch their march toward Jerusalem, they will destroy many peoples and ravage the land that lies before them -----

> Fire devours before them, and behind them a flame burns. The land is like the Garden of Eden before them, but behind them a desolate wilderness, and nothing escapes them. *Joel 2:3*

As this murderous Orc-army arrives in Jerusalem, they will ravage and rape -----

> For I will gather all the nations against Jerusalem to battle, and the city shall be taken and the houses plundered and the women raped. Half of the city shall go out into exile, but the rest of the people shall not be cut off from the city. *Zechariah 14:2*

These tremendously evil armies will inflict much pain and death in the city of Jerusalem.

Notes:

(Slides # 27 - 28)

THE WARRIOR REMNANT OF ISRAEL

However, there is a remnant of Jewish peoples that will not be defeated -----

> It will come about in all the land, declares the Lord, that two thirds in it will be cut off and perish; but the one third shall be left alive. *Zechariah 13:8*

Now it appears as if the many of the Israelites, including those in the Israel Defense Forces (IDF) will steadfastly resist this evil invasion.

➢ These would surely be Jews who have refused to pledge allegiance to the Antichrist and have no intention to surrender to this evil army even though they may be outnumbered by as many as 10,000 to 1.

➢ Perhaps many of them have not yet recognized Jesus as their Messiah but, to their credit, they steadfastly refused to take the "mark of the beast" and worship his "image."

However, for this heroic one-third remnant of God's chosen people who battle against these forces of evil, the hand of the Lord will be strong upon them:

> And I will put this third into the fire, and refine them as one refines silver, and test them as gold is tested. They will call upon my name, and I will answer them. I will say, 'They are my people'; And they will say, 'The Lord is my God.'" *Zechariah 13:9*

These are certainly the ones who the Lord would protect and anoint them with the "strength of David" in the midst of the battle.

> On that day the Lord will protect the inhabitants of Jerusalem, so that the feeblest among them on that day shall be like David, and the house of David shall be like God, like the angel of the Lord, going before them *Zechariah 12:8*

Notes:
_____
_____
_____
_____
_____
_____
_____
_____
_____

BREAK-TIME   **(Slides # 29 - 30)**

(Slides # 31 thru 34)
7th Bowl of God's Wrath
"Poured Out Into the Atmosphere"

As the battle continues, the 7th bowl is poured out into the air. Lightning and thunder are manifested worldwide followed by an unimaginable great earthquake that shakes the entire planet.

The Seventh Bowl

The seventh angel poured out his bowl into the air, and a loud voice came out of the temple, from the throne, saying, "It is done!" And there were flashes of lightning, rumblings, peals of thunder, and <u>a great earthquake such as there had never been since man was on the earth, so great was that earthquake.</u>

<u>The great city was split into three parts, and the cities of the nations fell</u>, and God remembered Babylon the great, to make her drain the cup of the wine of the fury of his wrath. <u>And every island fled away, and no mountains were to be found.</u>

And great hailstones, about one hundred pounds each, fell from heaven on people; and they cursed God for the plague of the hail, because the plague was so severe.
Revelation 16:17-21

This is also the day that the lord will war against these demonic armies where He says:

<u>Zechariah 14;3-5</u>

Then the Lord will go forth and fight against those nations, as when He fights on a day of battle. On that day his feet shall stand on the Mount of Olives that lies before Jerusalem on the east, and the Mount of Olives shall be split in two from east to west by a very wide valley, so that one half of the Mount shall move northward, and the other half southward.

And you shall flee to the valley of my mountains, for the valley of the mountains shall reach to Azal. And you shall flee as you fled from the earthquake in the days of Uzziah king of Judah. <u>Then the Lord my God will come, and all the holy ones with him</u>.

So on that coming day - the Lord brings about a mighty "7th bowl earthquake" in the midst of the battle - and causes the Mount of Olives to split in two - allowing His faithful remnant to escape - and separate themselves from the enemy - who is about to be destroyed:

Cities fall, mountains and islands disappear; and great hailstones weighing approximately 100 pounds each fall upon the masses of people.

- ➢ This plague of hailstones will kill tens of thousands causing a tremendous fear to arise among the ranks of the enemy.

- ➢ They become insanely scared and like the Orcs in the Lord of the Rings, they are at each others throats, slaughtering their own comrades for a great panic has gripped them:

> And on that day a great panic from the Lord shall fall on them, so that each will seize the hand of another, and the hand of the one will be raised against the hand of the other. *Zechariah 14:13*

These 100 pound hailstones which are poured out onto the heads of the enemy could also have been directed against the "principalities and powers of the air" since this 7th bowl is poured out into the air; the air being the abode of armies of evil powers and spirits.[13]

- Hailstones have historically been a part of the arsenal of weapons used by our Lord against His adversaries resulting in mammoth destruction and death.[14]

- Thus the 7th bowl being poured out into the air appears to represent destruction of the demonic forces of Satan as well as the earth.

This earthquake will be beyond man's comprehension. Isaiah presents us with an eye-opening description:

> *The earth is utterly broken, the earth is split apart, the earth is violently shaken. The earth staggers like a drunken man; it sways like a hut; its transgression lies heavy upon it, and it falls, and will not rise again.*
>
> *On that day the Lord will punish the host of heaven, in heaven, and the kings of the earth, on the earth. They will be gathered together as prisoners in a pit; they will be shut up in a prison, and after many days they will be punished.* Isaiah 24:19-22

Suddenly a voice is heard from the temple of God, "It is done."[15] This was the same voice that spoke those exact words some 2,000 years earlier when His work was completed on the Cross.[16]

- Now the judgments of God that have been poured out on the earth are complete. The time of His 2nd coming is being readied. The total redemptive purposes of God will now be consummated, both for salvation and for judgment.[17]

Notes:

_____
_____
_____
_____
_____
_____
_____

---

[13] Ephesians 2:2; 6:12
[14] Joshua 10:11; Ezekiel 38:18-22)
[15] Revelation 16:17
[16] John 19:30
[17] Ladd, George Eldon, *A Commentary on the Revelation of John*, (Grand Rapids: William E. Eerdmans Publishing Company, 1972) p.214

(Slides # 35 - 36)

THE COMING OF THE KING OF KINGS
(Revelation 19:11-21)

Many in the church of today believe that Jesus was a pacifist who preached "make love, not war."

➢ This is a popular belief among the numerous church-going Americans even though it is contrary to His assertion that:

> "Do not think that I have come to bring peace to the earth. I have not come to bring peace, but a sword. ....And whoever does not take his cross and follow me is not worthy of me. Whoever finds his life will lose it, and whoever loses his life for my sake will find it.
> *Matthew 10:34; 38-39*

In truth, our Lord Jesus calls His warrior-spirited disciples to "make war, because we love." Throughout the New Testament, He calls us time and again to the frontlines of the spiritual battlefield.

➢ This age is a time of warfare, and peace will never be a true reality in this world until every single enemy of the Lord, both fallen angels and sinful man, have been thrown into the lake of fire.

At His second coming, Jesus Christ rides down from heaven on a stallion of war rather than a donkey of peace.

➢ He is followed by a mighty army and His weapon is a great sword proceeding from His mouth which is the Word of God that will slaughter thousands of kings, generals, and mighty men among His enemies.

Key Points:

Has Jesus changed since His first coming? It is not His character or personality that have changed, but His mission.

➢ His first coming was to "seek and save what was lost"; not to condemn, but to save.[18]

➢ He was still the Warrior that challenged the false religions of Israel that was leading His people astray.

➢ He came to give mankind the opportunity to be separated from their sins before all sin has to be destroyed.

➢ Now His second coming is for the opposite purpose; to destroy rather than to save, to punish sin rather than to pardon it.

Notes:
_____
_____
_____

[18] Luke 19:10; John 3:17

(Slides # 37 - 38)

THREE MAJOR WEAPONS
USED AGAINST THE DEMONIC ARMIES

> **Up to this point in time, our Commander-in-Chief has employed three major weapons in this Great War against His enemies:**
>
> ➢ **One**: Seven bowls of God's wrath being poured out on the earth, into the seas, into fresh waters, on the sun, on the throne of the beast, into the Euphrates River, and finally, into the atmosphere above the earth.
>
> ➢ **Two**: Sending a spirit of fear and madness into the midst of the enemy forces causing them to fight among themselves. This is the same "sword of the Lord" that was used against His enemies when Gideon and his 300 man army came against the huge army of Midian.[19]
>
> ➢ **Three**: Equipping warriors among the Jewish people with a heart of David where they became like "a blazing pot in the midst of wood and a flaming torch among sheaves."[20]
>
> In summary, the armies of the Antichrist are currently experiencing unexpected resistance to their plans for conquest of the Kingdom of God, for they have suffered tremendous loss of life to this point.

Yet, millions of this enemy still remains alive and their hatred is raging. They have just slaughtered two-thirds of the Israelites and are intent on pursuing the remaining third which has escaped through the valley of the Mount of Olives that was split in two.

It is now time for the fourth and most powerful weapon in the arsenal of God to be revealed; a weapon which will completely annihilate the kings of the world and their armies.

"Look up, the Lion of Judah is coming with a His mighty army!"

> Behold, <u>he is coming with the clouds, and every eye will see him</u>, even those who pierced him, and all tribes of the earth will wail on account of him. Even so. Amen. "I am the Alpha and the Omega," says the Lord God, "<u>who is and who was and who is to come</u>, the Almighty."
> *Revelation 1:7-8*

Notes:

_____

_____

[19] Judges 7:20-22
[20] Zechariah 12:6

(Slides # 39 - 40)

THE COMING OF THE KING OF KINGS
Revelation 19:11

> The Rider on a White Horse
> Then I saw heaven opened, and **behold, a white horse!** The **one sitting on it is called Faithful and True**, and in righteousness he judges and makes war. ***Revelation 19:11***

Jesus is the Rider on a White Horse:

- The last time that Jesus came to Jerusalem, He came riding on donkey, a beast of burden, for He was about to suffer an agonizing death for those who are called into His kingdom. He was the King entering Jerusalem, but then His Kingdom was not of this world.
- Now He comes as a victorious warrior King to fight and destroy His enemies who have killed millions of His people over the last 6,000 years.

He is called "Faithful":

- Since the days of Abraham, the people of the Lord have been looking for His coming to establish the Kingdom of God upon the earth. Century after century elapses, and generation after generation passes away. <u>Dark and troublesome times continually engulfed His people and yet, He did not come.</u>

Yet, He did not come. Why?

- Many of His people who initially awaited His coming fell away and worshipped other gods and at the same time, persecuted those who remained faithful to the Lord. Both true faith and faithlessness had to be revealed among the hearts of mankind over time.

- Also, He did not immediately come because the number of His chosen people was not yet complete.

- At the time of His coming as the warrior King, it is complete. He is called the Faithful One to His people of faith.

He is also called "True":

- He is the true Messiah in distinction from all the powers that have ever opposed Him.

- Antichrist claimed that he was the promised messiah, but he was simply the last of many wannabes.

- Jesus Christ is the true Prophet, the true King, the true Word of God, and the true Son of God that the prophets of the Old Testament and the apostles of the New Testament have told us about.

Notes:

(Slides # 41 thru 43)

THE COMING OF THE KING OF KINGS
Revelation 19:12

> His **eyes are like a flame of fire**, and on his head are **many diadems (crowns)**, and he has a **name written that no one knows but himself.** *Revelation 19:12*

His eyes are like a "flame of fire:"

- The eyes of Jesus Christ penetrate into the darkness and the deepest corners of iniquity are completely visible to Him. The inner thoughts of all mankind are completely exposed to the one who's eyes are as a "flame of fire."

- Nothing remains hidden from the King when He comes for judgment.[21] He is gloriously focused on bringing the righteous judgment to the world.

There are many crowns upon His head:

- On His head John sees many "crowns" which are symbolic of all of the victories that our Lord has won in the historic battles against the forces of Satan.

- These multiple crowns also leave no doubt that Jesus Christ is the King of kings who has come to set up His eternal kingdom upon this earth.

He has a name written that no one knows but Himself:

- This appears to be a name given to Him by His Father; a name that exalts Him above every name in heaven and on earth.

- He also says to His conquering people, that He will give them a white stone with their name written upon it that no one knows except the one who receives it.[22]

- These names appear to be only known to the Father and His Son, so when we hear them throughout our eternal lifetime, we will know that He is calling us to His presence.

Notes:

_____
_____
_____
_____
_____

---

[21] Amos 9:1-4
[22] Revelation 2:17

(Slides # 44 thru 46)

THE COMING OF THE KING OF KINGS
Revelation 19:13

> *He is **clothed in a robe dipped in blood**, and the name by which he is called is **The Word of God**.*
> *Revelation 19:13*

He is clothed with a robe dipped in blood:

- ➢ Past victories in the Kingdom have also been very bloody as evidenced in both the old and new dispensations of this age.

- ➢ Yes, He is our beloved **Lamb of God** who sacrificed His life in order that His people may have eternal life. But, He is also our beloved **Lion of Judah** who has continued to walk with His people through the 'Valley of the Shadow of Death" for the past 6,000 years.

- ➢ This robe dipped in blood is spiritually symbolic of all those in the "Body of Christ" who also laid down their lives for the glory of the Lord.

He has other names including the "Word of God":

The Word of God Became Flesh
In the beginning was the Word, and the Word was with God, and the Word was God. He was in the beginning with God. All things were made through him, and without him was not any thing made that was made. In him was life, and the life was the light of men. The light shines in the darkness, and the darkness has not overcome it. *John 1:1-5*

And the Word became flesh and dwelt among us, and we have seen his glory, glory as of the only Son from the Father, full of grace and truth. *John 1:14*

- ➢ He is known to Himself and to His Father by His hidden name.

- ➢ He is known to the churches as the Faithful and True and as **the Word of God**.

- ➢ He is known to the world as King of kings and Lord of lords.

Notes:
_____
_____
_____
_____

BREAK-TIME   **(Slides # 47 - 48)**

(Slide # 49)

THE COMING OF THE KING OF KINGS
Revelation 19:14

Armies in heaven following Him on white horses.

> And the armies of heaven, arrayed in fine linen, white and pure, were following him on white horses. *Revelation 19:14*

- ➢ These certainly include of both His holy angels who have continually fought against Satan and his traitorous demons; as well as all those martyrs under the altar who refused to compromise and sacrificed their lives over the last sixty centuries.[23]

- ➢ Their numbers will also increase when those of the Lord's people who are alive on the earth at this time will be "caught up in the air" where they will join with their fellow soldiers on their return to the earth.[24]

- ➢ They wear robes of white linen which are representative of their holiness before God who gives them their robes.[25]

- ➢ They do not have armor or swords for they are not entering into the midst of the battle.

- ➢ They are present so that their Lord would be glorified among them for they are God's witnesses to an event that His people have been anticipating for centuries.[26]

Notes:
___

---

[23] Revelation 15:2-3; Mark 8:38; Luke 9:26; 1 Thessalonians 3:13; 2 Thessalonians 1:7-8
[24] 1 Thessalonians 4:17
[25] Revelation 6:11
[26] 2 Thessalonians 1:10

(Slide # 50)

THE COMING OF THE KING OF KINGS
Revelation 19:15

He treads the winepress of God the Almighty putting His enemies under His feet:

> ____He will tread the winepress of the fury of the wrath of God the Almighty. *Revelation 19:15*

- Jesus is the Commander-in-Chief who treads the winepress of the wrath of God.[27]

- The gathering of the grapes for the wine press takes place at Armageddon while the crushing takes place in this final battle.

This is also the time that David spoke of:

> David himself, in the Holy Spirit, declared, "'The Lord said to my Lord, Sit at my right hand, until I put your enemies under your feet.' *Mark 12:36*

This is also an event during the "harvest of the earth."

> And the winepress was trodden outside the city, and blood flowed from the winepress, as high as a horse's bridle, for 1,600 stadia (184 miles). *Revelation 14:20*

Notes:

---

[27] Revelation 14:20

(Slides # 51 thru 53)

THE COMING OF THE KING OF KINGS
Revelation 19:15

From His mouth comes a sharp sword:

> From his mouth comes a sharp sword with which to strike down the nations, and he will rule them with a rod of iron. ***Revelation 19:15***

- This sword is symbolic of the Word of God which proceeds from the mouth of Jesus Christ in tremendous power against His enemies.

- The same all-powerful Word that "spoke" all of creation into being will now destroy these last armies of all those who worshipped the creation, yet hated the Creator.

Now when the armies of Antichrist see the coming of the King of kings, they will gather together to make war against Him and against His holy army of angels and saints coming down from heaven.

- But they have no chance against them for immediately, like a mighty sword in the midst of great combat, the "**Word**" is shouted against the armies of Antichrist and……..:

> ….this shall be the plague with which the Lord will strike all the peoples that wage war against Jerusalem: their flesh will rot while they are still standing on their feet, their eyes will rot in their sockets, and their tongues will rot in their mouths. ***Zechariah 14:12***

- His enemies are completely consumed by the Word of His mouth; that same powerful Word that created the heavens and the earth.[28]

Notes:

---
[28] John 1:1-2; 14

(Slide # 54)

THE COMING OF THE KING OF KINGS
Revelation 19:17

Calling the "birds of the air" to the battlefield:

> Then I saw an angel standing in the sun, and with a loud voice he called to all the birds that fly directly overhead, "Come, gather for the great supper of God, to eat the flesh of kings, the flesh of captains, the flesh of mighty men, the flesh of horses and their riders, and the flesh of all men, both free and slave, both small and great." ***Revelation 19:17-18***

➢ The birds of the air are summoned by the voice of an angel to share in the victory by eating the flesh of the enemy that has been struck down by the Word of God.

➢ To give one's flesh to the birds of the atmosphere is expressive of the most complete defeat and shameful subjection of the enemy conceivable.[29]

➢ In the past, the enemy has humiliated the dead bodies of God's people by allowing the birds and the beasts to feed upon them.[30]

➢ Likewise Goliath threatened this same humiliation to young David, yet David responded by telling him that it was he and his entire army that would be killed and bodies given to the birds of the air.[31]

Notes:

_____

[29] Hoeksema, Herman, *Behold, He Cometh,* (Grand Rapids: Reformed Free Publishing Assn, 1969) p.634
[30] Psalm 79:1-2
[31] 1 Samuel 17:44-47

(Slides # 55 - 56)

THE COMING OF THE KING OF KINGS
Revelation 19:19-21

The Lake of Fire receives its first victims:

> And I saw the beast and the kings of the earth with their armies gathered to make war against him who was sitting on the horse and against his army. <u>And the beast was captured, and with it the false prophet who in its presence had done the signs by which he deceived those who had received the mark of the beast and those who worshiped its image. These two were thrown alive into the lake of fire that burns with sulfur.</u> And the rest were slain by the sword that came from the mouth of him who was sitting on the horse, and all the birds were gorged with their flesh.
> *Revelation 19:19-21*

➢ Antichrist and the false prophet are the first two that are thrown alive into the lake of fire.

➢ Antichrist's army has been totally slain and their flesh was gorged by the birds of the air. Yet their souls will suffer in hell while awaiting the final Day of Judgment; at which time they will follow their "beloved" Antichrist into the lake of fire which burns with sulfur.

➢ This is a lake that is probably composed of the same sulfurous fire that the Lord rained down on the cities of Sodom and Gomorrah.[32]

➢ This is a torturous lake that would not only be intensely hot, but with a foul putrid smell as well.

➢ Although, Satan himself, together with the angels of Death and Hades, plus all of sinful mankind will subsequently join them in this place of torment.

Notes:
_____
_____
_____
_____
_____
_____
_____
_____
_____

---
[32] Genesis 19:24

(Slides # 57 - 58)

THE COMING OF THE KING OF KINGS

In summary, the second coming of the Lord Jesus Christ is an all-out military attack by the armies of Heaven against the rebellious angels and against the armies of the nations.

- ➢ He will shout at the head of His armies. There is such passion in it, such anger, and such power. The flesh of the army of Antichrist will rot from their bodies while they are still standing on their feet. .

- ➢ Jesus is coming to judge the earth in righteousness. His shout is like the roar of a lion.

- ➢ He who died on the cross as a suffering servant is the same one who's coming back as a conquering King.

- ➢ As Jesus descends His feet will touch down on the Mount of Olives.

His chosen people appear to be this one-third remnant among the Jews who remained faithful in their hearts to the God of Abraham, Isaac, and Jacob:

And it shall come to pass that everyone who calls on the name of the Lord shall be saved. For in Mount Zion and in Jerusalem there shall be those who escape, as the Lord has said, and among the survivors shall be those whom the Lord calls. ***Joel 2:32***

(Slides # 59 - 60)

However, they still will not know who Jesus is - until the following takes place:

"And I will pour out on the house of David and the inhabitants of Jerusalem a spirit of grace and pleas for mercy, so that, when they look on me, on him whom they have pierced, they shall mourn for him, as one mourns for an only child, and weep bitterly over him, as one weeps over a firstborn. Zechariah 12:10

"In that day there will be a great mourning in Jerusalem ……. (Zechariah 12:11)

And when they ask the Lord Jesus, *'What are these wounds on your back?'* he will say, *'The wounds I received in the house of my friends.' Zechariah 13:6*

(Slides # 61)

The one-third remnant of the people of Israel that survived the Great War will come before Him on the Mount of Olives and when they recognize that their Messiah is truly Jesus Christ who was proclaimed by the Christian church, they will deeply mourn and weep.

- **Then the Lord Jesus will completely cleanse His beloved Jewish people who refused to take the "mark of the beast" or to worship the "image of the beast:"**

- **These are the ones who cried out for His coming' for Jesus had previously told the Jewish people:**

> For I tell you, you will not see me again, until you say, 'Blessed is he who comes in the name of the Lord.'" *Matthew 23:39*

Notes:

(Slide # 62)

THE NEXT SESSION:

First Read: Revelation 20:1-10

THE KINGDOM OF GOD REIGNING UPON THE EARTH

- The Millennial Age – A 1,000 Year Reign
- The Purpose of the Millennium
- Two Resurrections & the Resurrected Bodies of the Saints
- Non-Resurrected Peoples in the Millennium
- Resurrected Saints – Their Millennial Mission
- Satan Released & the Last World War
- Removal of Satan from the Earth
- Hades or Sheol – A Temporary Abode Awaiting Judgment

Additional Notes:

THE LAMB OF GOD - OUR TRUE "COMMANDER-IN-CHIEF"

The days are rapidly approaching when a tremendous separation will take place among mankind.

Yet, during this present era of warfare, He reigns as our Commander-in-Chief and His Name continues to be the battle cry for those warriors who fight daily for righteousness and truth.

His name is Jesus, Our Lord, Our King, Our Commander-in-Chief

- A truly mighty Leader who would never delegate assignments to His people that He Himself wouldn't readily embrace.

- A Commander that Christian warriors will readily follow not matter the danger or what costs have to be paid.

- These are warriors whose deepest desire is to hear Jesus welcome them with the following words when they enter into His presence:

> ……… 'Well done, good and faithful servant. You have been faithful over a little; I will set you over much. Enter into the joy of your master.' *Matthew 25:21*

THE KINGDOM OF GOD REIGNING UPON THE EARTH

(Revelation 20:1-10)

SESSION #13 – WORKBOOK
Intended For
"KINGDOM WARRIORS IN THE ARMY OF GOD"

Unveiling Mysteries in the "Book of Revelation"

Based upon the Book:
GOD'S ANOINTED WARRIORS
By
Dr. Donald Bell
Major USMC, Ret.

(Slides # 2 thru 5)
THE MILLENNIAL AGE
A 1,000 YEAR REIGN OF THE KING OF KINGS

> Then I saw thrones, and seated on them were those to whom the authority to judge was committed. Also I saw the souls of those who had been beheaded for the testimony of Jesus and for the word of God, and who had not worshiped the beast or its image and had not received its mark on their foreheads or their hands.
>
> They came to life and **reigned with Christ for a thousand years.** The rest of the dead did not come to life until the **thousand years** were ended. This is the first resurrection. Blessed and holy is the one who shares in the first resurrection! Over such the second death has no power, but they will be priests of God and of Christ, and **they will reign with him for a thousand years.** _Revelation 20:4-6_

(Slides # 6 - 7)
A-MILLENNIALISM

First, I want to briefly mention that many in the church have a problem understanding the reign of the Kingdom of God known as the Millennial Age; an age preceding the coming of the New Heavens and New Earth.

➢ **They have been taught that there is no actual future millennial kingdom and that these words in Revelation 20 are simply "spiritual."**

> **These "spiritual teachings" of the millennial period first surfaced with the influence of Greek Platonism on the church around the fourth century.**
>
> ➢ Platonism theology was mostly popularized by Augustine (350–430 AD), who was also a Greek. He was a popular theologian of the 5th century who spiritualized the biblical concept of the "new earth" being symbolic of a non-physical "spiritual heaven."
>
> ➢ Subsequently, the Roman Catholic Church came to embrace St. Augustine's view that human beings are better off without bodies and that Heaven is a disembodied spiritual state. (Certainly explains their priestly non-marriage philosophy).
>
> ➢ They teach that Satan has been bound since the resurrection of Jesus and that we are currently living in the millennial age. Additionally, several Protestant denominations also embrace this spiritualized millennial teaching.
>
> ➢ One only has to look at two-thousand years of continuing persecution and rampant false teachings within the church in order to understand that this is another deceptive teaching designed to put Christians to sleep while the real spiritual war is raging across the world.

My personal experience tells me that most Christians who adhere to views of a non-physical reign of Christ during a 1,000 millennial era are also among those who fail to discern the times for this present generation –

- A time of great tribulation and judgment coming upon the Christian church and our nation. They like to spiritualize these events also instead of facing the reality of truths clearly found in the prophetic book of Revelation.

(Slide # 8)

THE EARLY CHURCH FATHERS UNDERSTOOD THE TRUTH OF A PHYSICAL MILLENNIAL KINGDOM

Contrary to those "spiritualized" teachings, the majority of the early church fathers understood the millennial period to be an earthly, physical reign of the Lord Jesus Christ and His saints.

- They rightly understood the millennial era to be a thousand-year period which follows the defeat of the Antichrist-------yet precedes the Day of Judgment and the coming of the New Heavens and Earth.[33]

- **This is known as "historic (or classical) pre-millennialism"** and was embraced by our most prominent early church fathers, such as Ignatius, Polycarp, Irenaeus, Justin Martyr, Tertullian, etc.

- Other respected theologians such as Sir Isaac Newton, Charles Spurgeon, George Eldon Ladd, Merrill Tenney, Carl Henry, Francis Schaeffer, etc. also taught the truths of historic pre-millennialism.[34]

- They understood the millennial kingdom as being a time that the Old Testament prophets called the final redemption of Israel and that all the nations of the earth would be blessed through Israel because Jesus is reigning from Jerusalem.

- **A suggestion for those who have been taught differently: Read Revelation 19 and 20 without listening to anyone else.**

Notes:

---

[33] Gaebelein, Frank E., *The Expositor's Bible Commentary, Volume 12* (Grand Rapids: Zondervan Publishing House, 1981) p.578
[34] Pawson, David, *When Jesus Returns,* (London Sydney Auckland: Hodder & Stoughton, 1995) p.259

(Slide # 9)

The 1,000 year millennial period is bordered by two distinct judgments:

➤ The opening judgment (seven bowls of wrath being poured out) comes against all the nations, principalities, and powers that opposed Jesus Christ and His reign-----including many among the nation of Israel.

➤ The judgment that closes the millennial age is known as the final God-Magog war which completely erases evil from the creation forever.

Notes:
_____
_____
_____

(Slides # 10 - 11)

REMOVAL OF SATAN FROM THE EARTH
(Revelation 20:1-3)

Before the millennial kingdom can be established, the deceiver of the nations must be removed.

> Then I saw an angel coming down from heaven, holding in his hand the key to the bottomless pit and a great chain. And he seized the dragon, that ancient serpent, who is the devil and Satan, and bound him for a **thousand years**, and threw him into the pit, and shut it and sealed it over him, so that he might not deceive the nations any longer, until **the thousand years** were ended. After that he must be released for a little while. *Revelation 20:1-3*

Key Points:

➤ At this time, the human armies of Satan have been completely annihilated. His two human cohorts, Antichrist and the false prophet have already been thrown in the Lake of Fire.

➤ Now an angel from God has been dispatched from heaven with the authority to remove Satan himself from the earth so that he cannot deceive the nations during the coming millennial reign of Christ.

➤ **How will Satan be removed from the earth?** This mighty angelic representative of Almighty God will first seize Satan; then bind him with a great chain which will not be removed for a thousand years. He will then be thrown into a deep, bottomless pit.

➤ Additionally, it is quite probable that the demonic angels who were the dark agents of Satan for six thousand years are also imprisoned during this time: (2 Peter 2:4)

➤ **However, Satan's confinement is temporary**; at the end of the millennial period, he will again be released to go out among the nations to recruit an army for the final showdown between the Kingdom of the World and the Kingdom of God.

Note: Discuss with the group. Why wasn't Satan thrown in the Lake of Fire with the Antichrist?

(Slides # 12 - 13)

THE MILLENNIUM AGE – THE SEVENTH DAY OF REST

The 1,000 year millennial age will precede the coming of the new heaven and the new earth and will be a time when the earth is being "restored" for both God and man's eternal dominion.

Think of it like this:

> The time from Adam to Noah was a downward transition of the world away from a paradise in the Garden of Eden to a flood that destroyed life on earth.
>
> ➤ The time of the millennium is an upward transition from a world that has been devastated by the seven Bowl Judgments to a paradise restored – a new heaven and new earth.
>
> ➤ Thus, the millennium appears to be a 1,000 year transition between the life that we now have and the Garden of Eden-type paradise that comes with the new heaven and new earth.
>
> Now recall that the earth was created in six days and on the seventh day, God rested from all of His works; now these numbers are symbolic of many truths revealed in the Bible. **For example:**
>
> ➤ Six days of labor must be followed by a day of rest known as the Sabbath.
> ➤ The number six refers to man while the number seven symbolizes perfection and completion.
>
> **Additionally, when the apostle Peter described events that must take place before the end of the age, we learn that a single day with the Lord is as a thousand years to mankind.** [35]
>
> ➤ This prophecy of Peter's goes on to point out that "as the earth once perished by a Great Flood, so it will also perish by a great fire that is yet coming." [36]
>
> ➤ Likewise after the fires of the Armageddon war, there will dawn a new age known as the Millennium in which Jesus Christ, the Son of God will reign from a restored Jerusalem.

Notes:

_____
_____
_____
_____
_____
_____

---

[35] 2 Peter 3:8
[36] 2 Peter 3:4-8

(Slides # 14 - 15)

THE MILLENNIUM AGE – THE SEVENTH DAY OF REST

Also, there certainly appears to be a parallel between the six days of creation and the first six thousand years of human history.

> Key Points:
>
> ➢ These "sixes" may be described as a period of "labor"— six days of labor for the Creator and 6,000 years of labor for mankind.
>
> ➢ These "sevens" may be described as a period of "rest" --- one day of "rest" from labor for the Creator and 1,000 years of "rest" for mankind and the creation.
>
> ➢ Thus, the seventh 1,000 year period, known as the millennium, represents the Sabbath day of rest when equating the 7,000 years of mankind's history to the seven days of creation.
>
> **One of our very early church fathers by the name of Irenaeus was a man discipled by a close friend of the Apostle John.**
>
> ➢ Irenaeus also wrote a book called "Against Heresies" some fifty years after John recorded the Book of Revelation. In his book, Irenaeus says the following:
>
> *"As God views 1,000 years as a day and He created the earth in 6 days and rested on the 7th, so shall the earth last for 6,000 years and rest under the reign of Christ for the last 1,000 years".*
>
> ➢ Thus, Irenaeus, a man taught by a friend of the apostle John stated that Jesus Christ would return to reign on earth for one-thousand years which would represent a period of rest from six-thousand years of sinful, rebellious living in the world.
>
> **Finally, we should take note that the timeframe revealed in the bible puts us very close to the completion of six-thousand years since the time of creation.**

Notes:
_____
_____
_____
_____
_____
_____

BREAK-TIME   **(Slides # 16 - 17)**

(Slides # 18 - 19)

THE PURPOSE FOR THE MILLENNIUM

The Millennial Age will be a period of time that precedes the coming of the New Heaven and the New Earth; <u>a time when the earth is being "restored" for God and man's eternal dominion.</u>

Paul lays out a passage which provides some insights into the purpose of this one thousand year millennial period:

> For as in Adam all die, so also in Christ shall all be made alive. But each in his own order: Christ the first fruits, then at his coming those who belong to Christ. <u>Then comes the end, when he delivers the kingdom to God the Father</u> after destroying every rule and every authority and power. <u>For he must reign until he has put all his enemies under his feet.</u> **The last enemy to be destroyed is death.** *1 Corinthians 15:22-26*

Jesus Christ, the Son of God must reign until he puts all of His enemies under His feet.

➢ The Millennium is a period of His ruling where all evil will eventually be exposed and destroyed forever.

➢ Until that time, death still exists even though it has limited powers during the Millennium.

➢ At the end of the Millennium, death will be the last enemy destroyed and then, the kingdom is made ready for the Son to deliver it over to His Father.

The millennium is also a time when Jesus Christ is vindicated before the nation of Israel and the world that persecuted Him.

➢ Thus, the millennial age is a time for the rulership of Jesus; while the following age of the New Heaven and New Earth will be under the rulership of God the Father.

Jesus, as the <u>last Adam</u>, brings back obedience and fellowship to the Father, even as the <u>first Adam</u> broke that fellowship by disobedience.

Notes:
_____
_____
_____
_____
_____
_____

(Slides # 20 thru 23)

TWO RESURRECTIONS

> Then I saw thrones, and seated on them were those to whom the authority to judge was committed. Also I saw the souls of those who had been beheaded for the testimony of Jesus and for the word of God, and who had not worshiped the beast or its image and had not received its mark on their foreheads or their hands.
>
> **They came to life and reigned with Christ for a thousand years**. The rest of the dead did not come to life until the thousand years were ended. This is the first resurrection. Blessed and holy is the one who shares in the first resurrection!
>
> Over such the second death has no power, but they will be priests of God and of Christ, and they will reign with him for a **thousand years.** *Revelation 20:4-6*

Two resurrections are mentioned in these verses, one at the beginning of the millennial reign and one at the end. Now, it seems apparent throughout the church that all Christians who have died through the centuries are immediately raised up to heaven.

- For example, in Revelation 6 & 7 we are shown a great multitude standing before the throne and before the Lamb of God.
- Additionally, we are shown that the martyrs that have died for their faith are together under the altar before the throne of God.
- This all takes place before the millennial period. Thus, it appears that this first resurrection is not speaking about all the saints that have died since they are already in heaven.

> Key Points:
>
> **The first resurrection appears to be a <u>select group of saints</u> who lost their lives for their testimony of Jesus but will live and reign with Him on this earth for a thousand years.**
>
> - This group certainly consists of those who have been martyred for the gospel of Christ through the centuries, but it is probable that it is also for those who surrendered their lives totally for the kingdom, even though they were not physically martyred.
>
> - This will also include those who are alive at His coming and will be caught up into the air to join His holy army as they descend to the earth. They lived during the period of great tribulation, but refused to worship the Beast and did not receive his mark on their foreheads and hands. [37]
>
> - The first resurrection appears to be those who are the strongest and most mature warriors in the army of God. They will have leadership positions in His kingdom, helping prepare the world for the final stage of paradise.
>
> **Thus, the first resurrection appears to be a time when this select group of saints will receive their "resurrected bodies" and reign with Christ on earth during the millennial period.**

---

[37] 1 Thessalonians 4:17

The unbelievers of the human race will be among those of the second resurrection.

- The first resurrection is for a chosen group of the righteous only.
- The second resurrection is for those who denied the Lord during their life upon this earth.

The righteous ones that are not included in the "first resurrection" will be joyfully waiting in heaven during the millennial reign of Jesus and then descend with the heavenly Jerusalem at the end of the millennium. Then all those who are the bride of Christ will be united forever.

Yet, it should be our goal to make it to the first resurrection – if it means being physically martyred, so be it. If it means total dedication as if spiritually martyred, so be it.[38]

Listen to Paul's hope for a better resurrection:

> …..that I may know him and the power of his resurrection, and may share his sufferings, becoming like him in his death, that by any means possible I may attain the resurrection from the dead. ***Philippians 3:10-11***

- Paul obviously did not doubt his salvation. What he desired was to attain a higher level of resurrection and be part of the first resurrection.

The same principal applied to other heroes of the faith:

> ………others were tortured, not accepting their release, so that they might obtain a better resurrection; ***Hebrews 11:35 (NASU)***

Notes:

---

[38] Intrater, Keith, *From Iraq to Armageddon,* (Shippensburg: Destiny Image Publishers, Inc., 2003) p.154-155

(Slide # 24)

MILLENNIAL REIGN BEGINS—45 DAYS AFTER BOWL JUDGMENTS?

The following end-times prophecy in Daniel has been the subject of much speculation over the centuries. Perhaps the understanding of the coming millennial age might provide some insights into the blessings inherent within this prophecy.

> And from the time that the regular burnt offering is taken away and the abomination that makes desolate is set up, there shall be 1,290 days. Blessed is he who waits and arrives at the 1,335 days. But go your way till the end. And you shall rest and shall stand in your allotted place at the end of the days. *(Daniel 12:11-13)*

Key Points:

- Since Antichrist is to reign for 1,260 days from the time the abomination of desolation is set up in the temple mount, it would seem as if the additional 30 days represent the period of the "bowl judgments."

- If true, then the reign of Christ appears to begin on day 1,335, which is 45 days after the completion of the bowl judgments.[293]

- These 45 days may be a time when the earth is being prepared for the millennial kingdom and the first resurrection of those saints who will reign with Him takes place.

- This certainly would explain the blessedness associated with the 1,335 days.

Notes:

(Slide # 25)

RESURRECTED BODIES OF THE SAINTS

In order to get an idea of what our resurrected bodies will be like, we can look at Jesus' appearance when He walked the earth following His resurrection.

> Key Points:
>
> ➢ **He suddenly appears and disappears.**
>
> ➢ **The natural people** on earth will live in different locations and travel by normal means, while **the resurrected people** will be free to move into different locations as they are led by the Spirit of God.
>
> ➢ Like the resurrected Jesus, His resurrected saints will also walk, talk, and eat with those in the natural. They will have physical bodies which can be touched like those in the natural; <u>physical bodies that perform physical functions, but also have great supernatural capabilities.</u>
>
> ➢ Thus, the resurrected saints will be real people in real bodies; bodies that are incorruptible and eternally free from sin. <u>They are the first to receive their eternal, physical bodies.</u>
>
> ➢ These will be resurrected bodies of immortality with infinitely greater capabilities than the old physical bodies of this world that have been corrupted by sin.

(Slides # 26 - 27)

NON-RESURRECTED PEOPLE IN THE MILLENNIAL KINGDOM

Within the nations around the world will be innumerable peoples who survived the "Bowls of Wrath" and were not among the armed forces that had gathered at Armageddon and subsequently killed.

> **These will constitute the first generation of human beings living in the Millennial Kingdom.**
>
> ➢ These surviving people among the nations are in various stages of maturity. There will be babies, children, fathers and mothers, aunts and uncles, grandparents, etc.
>
> ➢ Prior to this time, the gospel of the Kingdom will have been preached throughout the nations, but many may not have heard or perhaps, did not understand.
>
> ➢ However, after witnessing His almighty power poured out across the earth, their understanding will have grown and there will no longer be any question in their minds that the God of Christianity is truly the one and only Almighty God.

> Many will have suffered tremendous grief at the loss of loved ones during this period and others are undoubtedly stricken with sickness from the plagues, but a period of the cleansing of the earth is about to begin.

> They may not understand who Jesus Christ is initially, since they will be in a state of shock and confusion, for the world is completely different from what they have been taught from birth.

> But, they will undoubtedly listen to the teachings which are about to go forth to the nations. These millennial evangelists are among those of the "first resurrection."

> Those who die during this millennial period will become part of the second resurrection at which time they will receive either eternal life or damnation.

Now Christians have always wondered about the destiny of peoples - who they believed - have never had the opportunity to hear the gospel message during their lifetime.

Key Points:

These would include:

> Ancient peoples in far countries, children who die at a young age, babies that have been aborted; these are examples of human lives that certainly never had the opportunity to know the Lord.

> Now Paul tells in Acts 17 that God overlooks times of ignorance, but since the resurrection of His Son, He calls all people everywhere to repent.

Okay - So what is their destiny? Well, consider this:

> Perhaps this millennial period is a time for those peoples to be resurrected into their natural bodies and experience life under the reign of Jesus Christ. If so, then these are peoples who comprise much of the natural population during the millennial era.

> Now, I know this is speculative, but perhaps it is possible.

Now, the natural people on earth will live in different locations and travel by normal means, while the resurrected people will be free to move into different locations as they are led by the Spirit of God.

Notes:

_____
_____
_____
_____
_____
_____

(Slides # 28 - 30)

THE MILLENNIAL AGE – A TIME OF RESTORATION

The thousand-year millennium period is a time designated by the Lord to bring about a restoration of all things.

> ➢ This will be a day to day restoring of the world to that condition that existed in the Garden of Eden-------a perfect world that our Lord calls, "very good."
>
> ➢ A time when many among mankind will walk in the fullness of Jesus Christ as sons and daughters of our Almighty Lord.
>
> ➢ A time when the entire creation, which has been groaning for six thousand years, will again rejoice over the righteous reign of the children of God:

…… the creation itself will be set free from its bondage to decay and obtain the freedom of the glory of the children of God. For we know that the whole creation has been groaning together in the pains of childbirth until now. And not only the creation, but we ourselves, who have the first fruits of the Spirit, groan inwardly as we wait eagerly for adoption as sons, the redemption of our bodies. *Romans 8:21-23*

The death and resurrection of Jesus Christ provided the means for the human race to be restored to our Father's design for us:

Repent, then, and turn to God, so that your sins may be wiped out, that times of refreshing may come from the Lord, and that he may send the Christ, who has been appointed for you — even Jesus. He must remain in heaven until the time comes for God to restore everything, as he promised long ago through his holy prophets. *Acts 3:19-21 (NIV)*

This is speaking of the millennial age!

Notes:

_____
_____
_____
_____
_____
_____
_____

(Slides # 31 - 32)

THE MILLENNIAL AGE – A TIME OF RESTORATION

Much of the detail concerning this restoration process is found in the prophetic books of the Old Testament. Some examples follow:

> **Restoring earth's dead waters:**
> A large river of fresh water will flow out of the Lord's millennial temple in Jerusalem so deep that one can only swim in it. It flows through the eastern part of the land and into the sea where it will change the seas into fresh water. These seas will again be populated with living creatures and every kind of fish.[39]

> **The animal kingdom will be restored back to the splendor of the Garden of Eden:**
> The wolf shall dwell with the lamb, and the leopard shall lie down with the young goat, and the calf and the lion and the fattened calf together; and a little child shall lead them. The cow and the bear shall graze; their young shall lie down together; and the lion shall eat straw like the ox.[40]

> **The earth will again yield tremendous fruit for His beloved people:**
> "Behold, the days are coming," declares the Lord, "when the plowman shall overtake the reaper and the treader of grapes him who sows the seed; the mountains shall drip sweet wine, and all the hills shall flow with it.[41]

> **Humans and animals will be united in love for one another:**
> The infant will play near the hole of the cobra, and the young child put his hand into the viper's nest. They will neither harm nor destroy on all my holy mountain, for the earth will be full of the knowledge of the Lord as the waters cover the sea.[42]

> **Length of life will be as the pre-flood era:**
> "Never again will there be in it an infant who lives but a few days, or an old man who does not live out his years; he who dies at a hundred will be thought a mere youth; he who fails to reach a hundred will be considered accursed.[43]

> **There will no slavery among mankind - each will reap the fruit of their own labors:**
> They shall not build and another inhabit; they shall not plant and another eat; for like the days of a tree shall the days of my people be, and my chosen shall long enjoy the work of their hands.[44]

These millennial peoples certainly will live long and healthy lives, but all will eventually be subjected to death since they have not yet been resurrected.

---

[39] Ezekiel 47:1-9
[40] Isaiah 11:6-7
[41] Amos 9:13
[42] Isaiah 11:8-9 (NIV)
[43] Isaiah 65:20 (NIV)
[44] Isaiah 65:22

(Slide # 33)

Finally, there is an remarkable parallel between the restoration of the earth during the millennial age and the sanctification process of "born-again" Christians. <u>In both cases, the spiritual regeneration precedes the physical.</u>

➢ That is, the earth requires the presence of Christ in order that it might be "born-again" and begin the process of physical restoration to its original state.

➢ Also, Christians require the "born-again" experience of the Holy Spirit before we can undergo the maturing process of restoration to our original state.[45] Pretty interesting!

Notes:

BREAK-TIME **(Slides # 34 - 35)**

---

[45] Pawson, David, *When Jesus Returns,* (London Sydney Auckland: Hodder & Stoughton, 1995) p.228

(Slides # 36 thru 38)

RESURRECTED SAINTS – THEIR MILLENNIAL MISSION

When Jesus was resurrected and appeared before various groups of people, He interacted socially with those who lived in human bodies.

- He talked with them, ate with them, cooked for them; they all fellowshipped together much like they did before His death.[46]

Key Points:

The resurrected saints of the millennial kingdom are going to interact with the peoples of all the nations from a heart of deep, passionate love. <u>A heart of Jesus!</u>

- These will be governing authorities, judges, evangelists, teachers, and advisors to the nations.

- They will be in positions of different levels of authority; depending on a person's gifting and proven record of dependability.[47]

- Jesus will be their King ruling from His temple in the capital city of Jerusalem.

Some will be on His cabinet overseeing various areas of government.

- Such as: the department of agriculture, commerce, transportation, etc. Some will be governors over provinces and some will be mayors over cities.

- Others will be in charge of leading worship in the temple. Still others will take the message of Jesus out to the peoples worldwide.

- Jesus will be teaching from the city of Jerusalem and His evangelists and teachers will be taking His message to the nations around the world.

These teachings will cause many peoples to say:

> "Come, let us go up to the mountain of the Lord, to the house of the God of Jacob, that he may teach us his ways and that we may walk in his paths." For out of Zion shall go the law and the word of the Lord from Jerusalem. He shall judge between the nations, and shall decide disputes for many peoples; and they shall beat their swords into plowshares, and their spears into pruning hooks; nation shall not lift up sword against nation, neither shall they learn war anymore.
> *Isaiah 2:3-4*

Notes:

_____

_____

---

[46] Luke 24; John 20
[47] Matthew 25:21; Luke 19:17

(Slides # 39 - 40)

THE MILLENNIAL GOVERNMENT

Unlike the original government established in the United States, the government ruling over the Kingdom of God will not be democratic.

> Key Points:
>
> ➢ It will be a glorious monarchy with Jesus Christ, the King of kings, ruling from His throne in the capital city of Jerusalem.
>
> ➢ His position of authority is not chosen by popular vote, but by the divine choice of Almighty God, our Father.
>
> **The Bible informs us that both Jesus Christ and His chosen leaders will rule over the nations with a "rod of iron."**
>
> ➢ This is indicative of strong and uncompromising rulership which will establish laws based upon the foundational truths of righteousness and holiness.
>
> ➢ The character of our Lord will be the ruling character in the lives of His sons and daughters who will live eternally under His kingship.

God's boundary lines for the nations which have been usurped by man may again be reestablished by this government:

> And he made from one man every nation of mankind to live on all the face of the earth, having determined allotted periods and the boundaries of their dwelling place, *Acts 17:26*

Most probably people groups will be broken down into seventy nations which is the number of the sons of God:

> When the Most High gave to the nations their inheritance, when he divided mankind, he fixed the borders of the peoples according to the number of the sons of God. *Deuteronomy 32:8*
>
> All the descendants of Jacob were seventy persons; .... *Exodus 1:5*

> **Nevertheless, during the millennial reign of this government, there will be many who would rather pursue the lusts of their hearts rather than the ways of the Lord.**
>
> ➢ Though they will outwardly obey the laws of the Kingdom; yet, within their hearts, they are hoping that a time will come when they can throw off the shackles of God's righteous laws and pursue their individual destiny.

These are those that our Lord describes as the:

> But as for the cowardly, the faithless, the detestable, as for murderers, the sexually immoral, sorcerers, idolaters, and all liars, their portion will be in the lake that burns with fire and sulfur, which is the second death." ***Revelation 21:8***

Notes:

_____
_____
_____
_____
_____
_____
_____
_____

(Slides # 41 - 42)

SATAN RELEASED & THE FINAL WORLD WAR

During the Millennium, the earth has been restored, peace reigns; inhabitants of the nations live with great joyous freedom. <u>And it is even going to get better.</u>

> Key Points:
>
> ➢ Although, before that time, the true people of God must be separated from those who would rather make their own laws and live life anyway they please.
>
> ➢ Yes, they are still in the world, but their hearts have not been visibly exposed. The Cain's exist right alongside of the Abel's.
>
> **Although the Lord Jesus Christ has visibly and physically reigned over mankind during the millennium, when the deceiver is set free from his prison, he will find the hearts of many to still be responsive to his seductions.**
>
> ➢ This makes it plain that sin is not rooted in poverty or inadequate social conditions; it is the rebelliousness of the human heart and its hatred for our Lord.
>
> ➢ The millennium age and the subsequent rebellion of men will prove that men cannot blame their sinfulness on their environment or unfortunate circumstances.[48]

---

[48] Ladd, George Eldon, *A Commentary on the Revelation of John*, (Grand Rapids: William E. Eerdmans Publishing Company, 1972) p.269

> Our Lord has always given mankind time to exercise their own free will and thereby choose their destiny. Then he allows circumstances to evolve whereby the intentions of the heart are visibly manifested.

> In the end, they will have no excuse beyond the sinfulness of their own rebellious heart when they stand before the Judgment Seat of our righteous and Almighty God.

Notes:
_____
_____

(Slides # 43 - 44)

SATAN RELEASED & THE FINAL WORLD WAR

As Satan is released, he will be allowed to move among the nations and tempt people to turn from the Lord exactly like he tempted Adam and Eve in the Garden.

> The rest of the imprisoned demonic hoards will undoubtedly be released with him and will be employed to deceive and rally mankind to rebel against the Kingdom of God.

> In the end of the 1,000 year millennium, Satan and his demonic allies build an army so numerous that "their number is like the sand of the sea."

The Defeat of Satan
And when the thousand years are ended, Satan will be released from his prison and will come out to deceive the nations that are at the four corners of the earth, Gog and Magog, to gather them for battle; their number is like the sand of the sea. ***Revelation 20:7-8***

Key Points:

This is the last of three major battles between the forces of light and darkness described in end-times prophecy:

> First, the battle of nations from Magog that comes against Israel. As mentioned in a previous session, I believe this to be the sixth seal event described in Ezekiel 38-39.

> The second battle is that known as Armageddon described both in Revelation 19 and various Old Testament prophecies. This comes at the end of the six-thousand year age of mankind and is followed by the second coming of Jesus to establish a 1,000 year millennial reign.

> The third battle is the final attempt by Satan and his followers to defeat the purposes of God at the end of the millennial reign of Christ. Here the enemies of God will be quickly consumed by fire. This will be followed by a day of final judgment.

(Slides # 45 - 46)

SATAN RELEASED & THE FINAL WORLD WAR

This last battle attempt to attack and seize Jerusalem, now the capital of the world, fails completely. In fact, the battle is never joined by the people of God on earth:

> And they marched up over the broad plain of the earth and surrounded the camp of the saints and the beloved city, but fire came down from heaven and consumed them, and the devil who had deceived them was thrown into the lake of fire and sulfur where the beast and the false prophet were, and they will be tormented day and night forever and ever. ***Revelation 20:9-10***

Key Points:

➢ The Kingdom of God no longer has need for armies; Joint Chiefs of Staff or a Secretary of Defense.

➢ Our Father in heaven sends down fire upon these enemy forces as they surround the city of Jerusalem; and they are completely consumed.

➢ The final Great War between the forces of light and darkness is also the shortest ever. The entire army of Satan is killed without the loss of a single human life among those in the Kingdom of God.

➢ This great climax will occur on the old earth before the new earth appears so that the entire world will witness the final victory of good over evil.

Many of us probably wonder why Satan would arise to lead this final rebellion.

➢ Did he not expect his defeat? Did he expect his last bid for earthly sovereignty to succeed? Was he self-deluded as well as the deceiver of nations? Did he really think he was stronger than God's people and therefore, God Himself?

➢ Or did he, knowing his fate was sealed, seek to take as many as he could to share in his ruin, in a last fit of frustrated rage? We may never know!

➢ However, we do know that the heart of Satan epitomizes the arrogant pride that refuses to recognize the righteousness of God even in the face of eternal judgment.

Notes:
_____
_____
_____
_____
_____

(Slides # 47 - 48)

HADES OR SHEOL – A TEMPORARY ABODE

Hades, (or Hell) in the **New Testament**, is the "temporary" holding place for the spirits of unrighteous men and women who have died in their sins.

➤ **It is not their eternal destiny**, but a place where they will experience continual unrest and torment until the coming of that day when they will be resurrected to stand before the Judgment Seat of Almighty God.

Sheol in the **Old Testament** is the equivalent of Hades however, prior to the resurrection of Jesus Christ; Sheol was the holding place for both the righteous and the unrighteous.

➤ It was composed of two entirely separate compartments that may be referred to as Paradise for the righteous and Torments for the unrighteous. These two compartments are visibly described in the parable of the Rich man and Lazarus.[49]

When Jesus laid down His life on the Cross, he first descended into Sheol, and released the righteous ones whose spirits had been awaiting His coming.

➤ Then the spirits of the righteous in Christ arose and accompanied Him into Heaven; although some of them appeared to many of the inhabitants of Jerusalem before they ascended into Heaven.[50] (These were undoubtedly the first witnesses to Jesus being the promised Messiah following His crucifixion.)

Notes:

---

[49] Luke 16:19-31
[50] Matthew 27:51-53; Ephesians 4:8-9; 2 Corinthians 12:1-4

(Slides # 49 - 50)

HADES OR SHEOL – A TEMPORARY ABODE

> **The spirits of our faithful brethren of the Old Testament dispensation could not go directly to Heaven until their sins had been completely cleansed by the shed blood of Jesus at the Cross; thus they had to wait in the paradise section of Sheol.**
>
> ➢ But now, all who die in Christ will ascend directly to Heaven and stand with all their brethren in the holy presence of our Almighty Lord.
>
> ➢ The spirits of the unrighteous dead will remain in Hades (hell) until the end of the millennial reign of Christ. At that time they will be resurrected to stand before the Judgment Seat of Almighty God who will then, determine their eternal destiny.

> **Another interesting scenario that certainly quite speculative: That is, some believe that Hades holds a remnant of people who are truly repentant but come to repentance only after experiencing the suffering of hell.[51]**
>
> ➢ Earlier, I mentioned the probability that many who have not had the opportunity to hear the true teachings of Scripture would be among those who may be resurrected during the millennial period; where they will be given an opportunity to freely choose their direction in life.
>
> ➢ The final judgment at the end of the Millennium which comes after an extended incarceration in Hades raises the possibility that God may consider that punishment as sufficient for some people.
>
> ➢ This sounds quite similar to those present day criminals who have been sentenced to prison for their crimes and subsequently have a "born again" experience. <u>The world has been taken from them; life has suddenly taken a different turn which opens one's heart to hear and receive the truth of God.</u> It took the punishment of imprisonment to open up the heart to repentance.
>
> ➢ Perhaps the parable of the Rich Man and Lazarus conveys the possibility that a period of suffering may bring true repentance.

The Bible does not answer this question and there is no reason to take a strong stance on it, one way or the other.

➢ However, if it is true that the dead in Hades are resurrected during the Millennial Age, they will certainly have the opportunity to manifest their true hearts.

➢ For when Satan and his demonic forces are released to raise a rebellious army designed to destroy the Kingdom of God, they can either choose to join with him or oppose him.

---

[51] Intrater, Keith, *From Iraq to Armageddon,* (Shippensburg: Destiny Image Publishers, Inc., 2003) p.204

(Slides # 51 - 52)

"ETERNALLY CONDEMNED" - OR - "ETERNALLY TORMENTED?"

It is understandable that all of mankind, both believers and unbelievers, have difficulties with the doctrine of eternal punishment.

- We all shrink from this teaching for none of us dare visualize how eternal punishment might be experienced by someone we know and love. <u>Yet, the Bible does not ignore this teaching and neither can we.</u>

- The reality of the fiery torments of hell should spur all of us to continually communicate this truth with great zeal and urgency.

- How long will the unrighteous be tormented in the Lake of Fire?

Traditional teachings stick to the view that Hell is a place of eternal, conscious torment.

- That is, a person who is sentenced to Hell is doomed to be painfully tormented forever and ever. Many respected theologians certainly believe this to be true.

- However, there are others who do not believe that sinners are eternally tortured but that, after completing their allotted period of torturous punishment, their souls disintegrate into what they perceive as the "second death."

- This is called the "conditionalist view" which sees sinners as being punished for a period of time before dying; as opposed to the "traditionalist view" who see sinners as suffering eternal punishment.

The Conditionalist teaches that "eternally condemned" means that sinners do suffer for a period of time in the Lake of Fire, but eventually their soul disintegrates in nothingness; however, the memory of their tormenting punishment is never forgotten.

- At times, the Bible certainly does appear to say the souls of sinners suffer eternally while in other places it is evident that there are varying degrees of suffering; some suffer more than others.

- Does that mean some places are hotter than others or do some suffer longer than others?

- What the Conditionalist view does is magnify the justice of God (each doomed sinner receives precisely what he or she deserves and nothing else), the mercy of God (even the worse sinner finally perishes forever), and the holiness of God (His wrath is real, but it is measured with exact precision in keeping with His own character)."

Notes:
_____
_____

(Slide # 53)

THE NEXT SESSION:

First Read: Revelation 20:11-15; Revelation 21 & 22)

THE GREAT WHITE THRONE JUDGMENT
&
THE NEW HEAVEN AND THE NEW EARTH

- The Day of Judgment

- Judgment Day – Who will be Judged?

- The Book of "Works" and the Book of "Life"

- Lake of Fire – The Permanent Abode of the Ungodly

- The New Heaven & New Earth

- The New Jerusalem

- Heaven: Boring or Exciting?

- Life on the New Heaven & New Earth

- "Behold, I Am Coming Soon"

- A Final Warning

Additional Notes:

THE LAMB OF GOD - OUR TRUE "COMMANDER-IN-CHIEF"

The days are rapidly approaching when a tremendous separation will take place among mankind.

Yet, during this present era of warfare, He reigns as our Commander-in-Chief and His Name continues to be the battle cry for those warriors who fight daily for righteousness and truth.

His name is Jesus, Our Lord, Our King, Our Commander-in-Chief

➢ A truly mighty Leader who would never delegate assignments to His people that He Himself wouldn't readily embrace.

➢ A Commander that Christian warriors will readily follow not matter the danger or what costs have to be paid.

➢ These are warriors whose deepest desire is to hear Jesus welcome them with the following words when they enter into His presence:

> .... 'Well done, good and faithful servant. You have been faithful over a little; I will set you over much. Enter into the joy of your master.' *Matthew 25:21*

GREAT WHITE THRONE JUDGMENT & THE NEW HEAVEN & NEW EARTH

(Revelation 20 – 21 - 22)

SESSION #14 – WORKBOOK
Intended For
"KINGDOM WARRIORS IN THE ARMY OF GOD"

Unveiling Mysteries in the "Book of Revelation"

Based upon the Book:
GOD'S ANOINTED WARRIORS
By
Dr. Donald Bell
Major USMC, Ret.

(Slides # 2 - 3)

The events which will be addressed in this presentation are intended to provide God's anointed Christian warriors with insights into the coming Kingdom of Almighty God.

➢ A Kingdom which will bring closure to the 1,000 year millennial reign of His Son, the Lord Jesus Christ.

(Slides # 4 thru 8)

THE COMING DAY OF JUDGMENT

This coming Day of Judgment will be such a glorious event for all those who have been burdened throughout the centuries for it will be a day when righteousness and justice will be manifested forever and ever.

First Purpose for the Day of Judgment:

> ➢ Everyone will finally understand that God is truly omniscient and omnipresent; that is, He knows our every thought and the true motive behind our every action throughout each of our individual lifetimes.
>
> ➢ Nothing has ever taken place in the actions, minds, or hearts of any man or woman that is hidden from our all-knowing and always-present God who initially created us in His image.
>
> ➢ His eyes have not only been upon us outwardly, but He also sees into our minds and hearts during every second of our entire lives.

For example:

> Nothing in all creation is hidden from God's sight. Everything is uncovered and laid bare before the eyes of him to whom we must give account. *Hebrews 4:13*

> The eyes of the Lord are everywhere, keeping watch on the wicked and the good. **Proverbs 15:3**

> Death and destruction lie open before the Lord; how much more the hearts of the children of man! **Proverbs 15:11**

> And all the churches will know that I am he who searches mind and heart, and I will give to each of you as your works deserve. **Revelation 2:23**

One by one, every man and woman who ever lived will stand before the Great White Throne of Almighty God.
➢ And as the true hearts of each person become visible to all (for we will all be witnesses), then all will come to understand His righteousness that determines man's eternal destiny.

In summary, the Day of Judgment will display the perfect righteousness of God in the determination of each person's destiny.

Second Purpose for the Day of Judgment:

It is to reveal the degree of rewards as well as the degree of punishments for every person who ever lived since the foundation of the world.

➢ The degrees of reward or punishment are related to the lives that people have lived and - the knowledge that they have received throughout their lifetime. All of this will be revealed to the world when the "books" are opened before the Throne.

➢ The bible reveals that some rewards are greater than others AND some punishments are more severe than others.

Third Purpose for the Day of Judgment:

It is to execute God's judgment on each person before the entire creation.

➢ This is a universal judgment over all of mankind; a judgment passed upon the wicked and the righteous on the same day.

➢ All will be judged; and this judgment brings forth varying degrees of rewards to His people as well as varying degrees of punishments to His enemies.

➢ For example - Are they truly sons and daughters of God - where they will live together with Him on the New Heaven and New Earth-------OR will they be cast into the Lake of Fire from which they will never depart?

FROM THIS JUDGMENT, THERE SHALL BE NO APPEAL, IT IS EVERLASTING.

Notes:
_____
_____
_____
_____
_____
_____
_____
_____
_____
_____
_____
_____

(Slide # 9 thru 11)

JUDGMENT DAY – WHO WILL BE THE JUDGE?

> Then I saw a great white throne and him who was seated on it. From his presence earth and sky fled away, and no place was found for them. **Revelation 20:11**

➢ It appears as if the One who sits on the Great White Throne, from whose presence both the heavens and earth flee away, is Almighty God, the creator of all life, and the Father of our Lord Jesus Christ.

Yet, God, the Father, judges the world in and through His Son.

> The Father judges no one, but has given all judgment to the Son, that all may honor the Son, just as they honor the Father. Whoever does not honor the Son does not honor the Father who sent him. **John 5:22-23**

➢ **When the entire creation appears before the Throne on the great Day of Judgment, it is unquestionable that the Father will personally be present sitting on the Great White Throne.**

➢ **Jesus Christ is the Son of Almighty God, but He also has a human nature and He is the Father's representative to the entire world. The Father's authority has been given to His Son:**

➢ **Therefore, we shall all stand before the Father and His Son, who also sits on His throne at the right hand of the Father. And in the Son's hands, will be the Book of Life.**

This will be the Day when we hear the following words of Jesus spoken in finality before each and every person.

> So everyone who acknowledges me before men, I also will acknowledge before my Father who is in heaven, but whoever denies me before men, I also will deny before my Father who is in heaven. **Matthew 10:32-33**

Notes:

_____
_____
_____
_____
_____
_____
_____

(Slides # 12 thru 18)

JUDGMENT DAY – WHO WILL BE JUDGED?

Now again, who will stand before the Great White Throne in judgment?

Answer:

> And I saw the dead, great and small, standing before the throne, and books were opened. Then another book was opened, which is the book of life.
> And the dead were judged by what was written in the books, according to what they had done.
> And the sea gave up the dead who were in it,
> Death and Hades gave up the dead who were in them, and they were judged, each one of them, according to what they had done. **Revelation 20:12-13**

Thus, all of mankind, from Adam to the very last person who ever lived; all shall appear before the final judgment seat.

- ➤ Cain and Abel, Moses and Pharaoh, Elijah and Jezebel, David and Goliath, John the Baptist and Herod who beheaded him, Apostle Paul and the Emperor Nero, Martin Luther and all the Catholic Popes,
- ➤ Charles Spurgeon and Karl Marx, Adolph Hitler and Corrie Ten Boom, Stalin, Mao and the millions of Christians slaughtered under their rulership, Bill Gates, Hollywood celebrities and the homeless, the Clinton's and the Reagan's, the Obama's, the Biden's, and the Trump's, great and small, kings and slaves, rich and poor, young and old; all will appear before the Judgment Seat of Almighty God.
- ➤ Bodies of the dead which were never retrieved such as suicide bombers, those lost at sea, those devoured by beasts, those that have been dead for thousands of years; all will be resurrected and their bodies and souls will be reunited.

And they will stand before the Judgment Seat of Almighty God.

This may also be the day that the rebellious angels that aligned with Satan against the Lord will also be judged:

> And the angels who did not stay within their own position of authority, but left their proper dwelling, he has kept in eternal chains under gloomy darkness until the judgment of the great day— **Jude 6**

The Final Judgment Occurs:

> "When the Son of Man comes in his glory, and all the angels with him, then he will sit on his glorious throne. Before him will be gathered all the nations, and he will separate people one from another as a shepherd separates the sheep from the goats.
>
> And he will place the sheep on his right, but the goats on the left.
> Then the King will say to those on his right, 'Come, you who are blessed by my Father, inherit the kingdom prepared for you from the foundation of the world. **Matthew 25:31-34**

> "Then he will say to those on his left, 'Depart from me, you cursed, into the eternal fire prepared for the devil and his angels. **Matthew 25:41**

In summary –
- Following this final resurrection, mankind will appear one-by-one before the Throne; the books will be opened and the thoughts and deeds of every living being will be disclosed to every generation throughout the history of mankind.

- **As the final judgment is pronounced on each person, they will either go to stand with the righteous at the right hand of God or with the unrighteous on the left.**

Notes:

BREAK-TIME (Slides # 19 - 20)

(Slides # 21 - 22)

JUDGMENT ACCORDING TO WORKS

We will all be judged by our works during our lifetime - as we see in verse 12:

> And I saw the dead, great and small, standing before the throne, and books were opened. Then another book was opened, which is the book of life.
> And the dead were judged by what was written in the books, according to what they had done.
> **Revelation 20:12**

All the works of mankind must be revealed in their true ethical character. All of our works in their proper light shall be exposed before God, before the world, and before ourselves.

➢ The reason for this is that God must be justified when He judges and that He has always declared righteous judgments throughout history no matter whether mankind agreed or disagreed with the consequences of His judgments.

> **This Day of Judgment is at the end of an age when the thoughts and intents of every heart is exposed and the righteousness of Almighty God cannot be disputed by either His people or His enemies.**
>
> ➢ Many times throughout our life, we see evil people getting away with rape and murder and we wonder why God does not immediately pour out His wrath upon these people.
>
> ➢ But on this Day, every mouth will be silenced and all shall acknowledge the perfect justice of God in both His righteousness and His timing.
>
> ➢ No one shall be dissatisfied with His judgments. Satan and his demonic world, as well as God's people and heaven's angels will have to acknowledge that God's judgments are perfectly righteous.

Although believers have nothing to fear from the judgment, the realization that everything we have said, thought, and done will be revealed before the entire world. This should provide us with a strong and continuing incentive to fight against sin.

Notes:
_____
_____
_____
_____
_____
_____
_____

(Slides # 23 - 26)

WHAT WILL BE THE STANDARD BY WHICH MEN WILL BE JUDGED?

The standard is the revealed will of God in each of our lives, but it is not the same for all. Some have received greater revelation of the will of God than others.

➢ Those who have received a greater revelation of God's will, have greater responsibilities.

➢ All of mankind, even those who are ignorant of the Bible do know that God is their Creator even though they refuse to accept the truth.

This is revealed in Romans 1 where we read:

> The wrath of God is revealed from heaven against all ungodliness and unrighteousness of men, who by their unrighteousness suppress the truth.
>
> ➢ For what can be known about God is plain to them, because God has shown it to them.
>
> ➢ For his invisible attributes, namely, his eternal power and divine nature, have been clearly perceived, ever since the creation of the world, in the things that have been made. So they are without excuse.
>
> ➢ For although they knew God, they did not honor him as God or give thanks to him, but they became futile in their thinking, and their foolish hearts were darkened. **Romans 1:18-21**

This is often referred to as our conscience.
➢ That inner sense of right and wrong that is the essence within the soul of every human being for mankind was created in the "image of God."

The reason the Bible teaches that the final judgment will be according to works, even though salvation cannot be earned by works, is the intimate connection between faith and works.

Faith will always reveal itself in works; as good works are the visible evidence of true faith. If the faith is genuine, the works will be there:

> As the body apart from the spirit is dead, so also faith apart from works is dead. **James 2:26**

Notes:
___
___
___
___
___
___
___

(Slides # 27 thru 29)

THE "BOOK OF WORKS" & THE "BOOK OF LIFE"

All believers shall stand before the Great White Throne on Judgment Day and as the books are opened, we shall see our sins as they have never fully been seen before.

- ➢ On that day we shall all understand that even some of our best works were defiled by sin and therefore, we have no hope for eternal life based upon our perception of "good works."

- ➢ However, there is another glorious book and it is held in the hands of Jesus Christ standing at the right side of His Father.

- ➢ This is the Book of Life which contains the names of all His chosen ones who are redeemed by the blood of their Lord and Savior.

- ➢ Thus, following the exposure of one's works, the Book of Life will then be opened to determine if their name is recorded.

  If so, then their sins are removed from the presence of God as far as the "east is from the west."

- ➢ **Then we will be called to stand on the right side of our Lord and Savior, Jesus Christ.**

This is the fulfillment of His promise when He said:

> The one who conquers will be clothed in white garments, and I will never blot his name out of the book of life. I will confess his name before my Father and before his angels.
> **Revelation 3:5**

The great and final decision in judgment shall be whether or not one's name is written in the Book of Life!

> And if anyone's name was not found written in the book of life, he was thrown into the lake of fire.
> **Revelation 20:15**

In summary then - the significance of the Day of Judgment can be summarized in the following three observations:

1. **This Day reveals to all, that salvation and eternal blessedness is dependent on one's relationship to Jesus Christ.**

2. **This Day underscores man's accountability for his life - and the opportunities that God has provided to allow one to accept or reject - His holy authority over life.**

3. **This Day is the final and decisive conquest of all evil - and the great revelation of the victory of the Lamb who was slain and rose again.**

At the close of this Day of Judgment, the will of God for this age will be perfectly complete.
(AMEN)

(Slides # 31 thru 36)

GOD'S PURPOSE FOR ALLOWING EVIL IN HIS CREATION

At the end of this Day of Judgment, the Tree of the Knowledge of Good and Evil, which was introduced in the Garden of Eden, will have fulfilled its purpose.

<u>Now, what do I mean by this?</u>

➤ In my video session entitled "Spiritual Warfare and the Problem of Evil" I presented eight wondrous truths that evolved from the fall of mankind in the Garden of Eden.

A brief summary of these eight glorious truths are as follows:

1. Adam's fall revealed that mankind had free-will, but did not yet have a true heart of love for God, his Creator.
2. The fall of mankind demonstrates our dependency upon God - that is needed to conquer death and to sustain life.
3. The depth of our Lord's love would not have been seen and understood without the Fall and thus, we would not have truly known Him as He desired for us.
4. Knowledge of good and evil is necessary in order to truly understand - and fully appreciate the perfect world - in which believers - will eternally live.
5. The fall provided the opportunity to bring forth Kingdom Warriors empowered by God to fight the battles against the powers of evil for the purpose of delivering numerous peoples unto salvation who have been enslaved by Satan. These are certainly among those who receive the greater rewards.
6. The fall of mankind provided the opportunity for our heavenly Father to introduce His Son who would reflect God's personality in a way hat mankind can truly understand. We would not have truly come to know Him without the Fall for Jesus would not have become a man.
7. Those who are "born again" by the blood of Christ have a new relationship with God – that was not available to Adam – in his original state. This is a relationship of family – purchased by the blood of God Himself. **Mankind no longer appears simply, in the image of God, as Adam was before the Fall; we have been born again and our identity is now - sons and daughters of Almighty God, who is now, not only our Creator but, our glorious Father.**
8. Those of mankind who choose to believe and follow the Lord – will one day be united together, forever – in the likeness of His Son.

This is the fulfillment of the prayer of Jesus to His Father

> Dear Father - The glory that you have given me I have given to them, that they may be one even as we are one, I in them and you in me, that they may become perfectly one, so that the world may know that you sent me and loved them even as you loved me.
>
> John 17:22-24:

Thus, those whose names are written in the Book of Life can say:

> *"Thank you Father, for allowing the Fall to occur - which has provided us with the opportunity to grow more and more into the likeness of Your glorious Son through our growing understanding of good and evil; and to allow us to stand against the darkness of evil as we allow the Light of Jesus Christ to shine through us."*

And at the close of the Day of Judgment, the sons and daughters of our Almighty Father may eat from the Tree(s) of Life forever and ever.

BREAK-TIME   **(Slides # 37 - 38)**

(Slides # 39 thru 44)

LAKE OF FIRE – THE PERMANENT ABODE OF THE UNGODLY

The Lake of Fire (Hell) is described in various sections of the Bible as a place of
- Darkness, / fiery torment, / sorrow, / bitterness / disgrace, / and everlasting contempt.

None of the characteristics of the Lord - which we take for granted in this life - will be available in Hell.
- For the Lord's presence is no longer available!

For hell is a place that is absent of the presence of God. That is:

> - Light will no longer exist - only darkness!
> - Love will no longer exist - only anger and hate!
> - Joy will no longer exist - only depression!
> - Peace will no longer exist - only restless turmoil!
> - For the Lord's presence is no longer available!

Who are those who will be thrown into the Lake of Fire?

> But as for the cowardly, the faithless, the detestable, as for murderers, the sexually immoral, sorcerers, idolaters, and all liars, their portion will be in the lake that burns with fire and sulfur, which is the second death." **Revelation 21:8**

The defeat of Death:

> Then Death and Hades were thrown into the lake of fire. This is the second death, the lake of fire. **Revelation 20:14**

Death lost much of its power when Jesus was raised from the dead and lost even more throughout the millennial period. But now, **Death is the last enemy to be defeated.**

Death appears as the evil angel who is the rider on the pale horse and Hades as another evil angel who follows right behind him:

> And I looked, and behold, a pale horse! And its rider's name was Death, and Hades followed him. And they were given authority over a fourth of the earth, to kill with sword and with famine and with pestilence and by wild beasts of the earth. **Revelation 6:8**

Death & Hades are:

> **The two most powerful angelic beings in the demonic realm under the rulership of Satan.**
>
> - Now Satan, together with his cohorts the angel of Death, and the angel of Hades will all join the Antichrist and the false prophet in this horrendous, putrid, and tormenting Lake of Fire.
>
> - The Lake of Fire is an eternal demonstration of the wrath of God.
>
> **God's righteous power and glory can be demonstrated both in blessing and in punishment.**

(Slides # 45 & # 46)

THE NEW HEAVEN & NEW EARTH

Judgment is now complete; the time has arrived that all of the people of God have been yearning for since the Fall of Adam. That is:

The Coming of the New Heaven and the New Earth:.

> Then I saw a new heaven and a new earth, for the first heaven and the first earth had passed away, and the sea was no more. **Revelation 21:1**

> And I heard a loud voice from the throne saying, "Behold, the dwelling place of God is with man. He will dwell with them, and they will be his people, and God himself will be with them as their God. He will wipe away every tear from their eyes, and death shall be no more, neither shall there be mourning nor crying nor pain anymore, for the former things have passed away." **Revelation 21:3-4**

This will be so much more glorious than the Garden of Eden.

- There, it was God walking with man whom He created in His image.

- Here, it is our Almighty Father living among His sons and daughters who have been truly "born again" - by the blood of the conquering Lamb of God.

- This is a picture of a great and glorious family who will live together forever and ever in the Kingdom of God; a family which will reign over the entire universe.

Notes:
_____
_____
_____
_____
_____
_____
_____
_____
_____
_____

(Slides # 47 thru # 50)

NEW HEAVEN & NEW EARTH – A RESTORATION – NOT A CREATION

A New Heaven and New Earth do not mean that the present heavens and earth have been completely annihilated and replaced.

- From the very beginning, God promised mankind nothing less than the Earth itself as his proper habitation and inheritance.
- When man sinned, his dominion over the Earth was not taken away but, the Earth over which he now ruled was under a curse.

> And he who was seated on the throne said, "Behold, I am making all things new." Also he said, "Write this down, for these words are trustworthy and true." **Revelation 21:5**

The New Heaven and New Earth is a "restoration" of the old, not a "creation" of a new.

Consider the following three points:

1. Here the word "new" is the Greek word **"kainos;"** which communicates that it is new in nature and not a new creation.

   - If it was "new" in origin, then the Greek word **"neos"** would have been used.

   - This is a **"kainos"** heaven and **"kainos"** earth that is revealed in these passages.

   Thus, the earth is being perfectly restored – to the point where our Lord, who created both the heavens and the earth, can once again say "It Is Good!"

2. **All of creation awaits the coming restoration:**

The Book of Romans informs us that this present creation is eagerly waiting the revealing of the sons of God so that it may be free from its bondage of decay and death.

> For the creation waits with eager longing for the revealing of the sons of God. For the creation was subjected to futility, not willingly, but because of him who subjected it, in hope that the creation itself will be set free from its bondage to decay and obtain the freedom of the glory of the children of God.
> For we know that the whole creation has been groaning together in the pains of childbirth until now. And not only the creation, but we ourselves, who have the first fruits of the Spirit, groan inwardly as we wait eagerly for adoption as sons, the redemption of our bodies.
> **Romans 8:19-23**

3. Consider our very selves.

> - Our resurrected bodies are not a new creation; we are **REBORN** into new bodies in which sin can no longer enter.
>
> - We will not be a totally new set of human beings, but people of God who formerly lived lives upon the earth.
>
> - Unrighteousness will never again be found in us and likewise, unrighteousness existing in the old creation will never be found in the restored creation.
>
> - The New Earth will still be as much Earth as the new us - will still be us.
>
> - The earthly beauty that we now see won't be lost, but will become even more beautiful following the restoration of the Heaven and Earth.
>
> - All of the old Earth that matters will be drawn into Heaven, to be part of the New Earth.
>
>   **GOD IS NO MORE DONE WITH THE EARTH THAN HE'S DONE WITH US.**

Notes:

(Slides # 51 thru # 54)

THE NEW JERUSALEM

The New Heaven and New Earth will need a Capitol City from which to govern the whole universe.

> And I saw the holy city, New Jerusalem, coming down out of heaven from God, prepared as a bride adorned for her husband. **Revelation 21:2**

This is the New Jerusalem, which is the promised restoration of the beloved City of God.

➤ This city will be a place from where God the Father and His Son will dwell with reborn sons and daughters - as well as the beloved angels - who have been guardians of His people throughout the age of mankind.

This is a place that was being prepared for His people when Jesus first ascended to heaven over two thousand years ago where He promised us that:

> In my Father's house are many rooms. If it were not so, would I have told you that I go to prepare a place for you? And if I go and prepare a place for you, I will come again and will take you to myself, that where I am you may be also. **John 14:2-3**

There will be no temple in the New Jerusalem:

> And I saw no temple in the city, for its temple is the Lord God the Almighty and the Lamb. And the city has no need of sun or moon to shine on it, for the glory of God gives it light, and its lamp is the Lamb. **Revelation 21:22-23**

The City is also described as the Bride of Christ which appears to indicate that the all of His sons and daughters are within its walls as it descends to the New Earth.

The beauty of this City is far beyond our most incredible imaginations.

➤ A City of pure gold, transparent as glass, with twelve foundations adorned with every kind of jewel, and with twelve gates, each composed of a single pearl.

➤ Each of the twelve gates is inscribed with the names of the twelve tribes of Israel; and the twelve foundations under the walls of the city are inscribed with the names of the twelve apostles of the Lord Jesus.

➤ Thus, all His sons and daughters, from both the old and new dispensations have entered through the gates - and live within these walls - surrounding the City of New Jerusalem.

Notes:
_____
_____
_____
_____
_____

- ➤ **This City is designed as a perfect square measuring approximately 1,400 miles both in length and in width, with walls 216 feet high.**

- ➤ This is the distance from the Canadian border to the Gulf of Mexico and from the Atlantic Ocean westward to Colorado.

- ➤ A River of Life flows out from the Throne of God throughout the city and through the gates into the world beyond.

- ➤ Trees of Life, which were denied to Adam following his fall, now grow on both sides of this River and are accessible to all of His people.

- ➤ There will never again be any need for sun or moon, for the glory of the Lord provides a great and glorious light forever.

QUITE AN AMAZING PICTURE!

Notes:

(Slides # 55 thru # 57)

THE NEW HEAVEN & EARTH – BORING OR EXCITING?

Heaven has always been dominant in the thoughts and lives of all of mankind since the beginning of time. Everyone strives to imagine what life will be like in the eternal realm.

> ➤ The Heaven that Jesus described is not some spiritual realm of disembodied spirits.
>
> ➤ Such a place could never be home for us, because human beings were not created for a non-physical existence. Human beings are by nature physical as well as spiritual.
>
> ➤ Our home that we love is the place that God made for us: The Earth. We were made from the earth and for the earth. Earth is our home.
>
> **The coming of the New Heaven and New Earth is a real event that will visibly combine both the physical and spiritual worlds together forever.**

The presence of our Lord is currently in Heaven, but at the end of the age, when all evil has been cast away, God will unite the Heavens and the Earth under the headship of Jesus Christ, and His people will have access to His presence forever and ever.

> ➤ Everything good, enjoyable, refreshing, fascinating, and interesting originates with God. Outside of God's presence, there is no joy.
>
> ➤ On the New Earth, our Lord will give us renewed minds and marvelously constructed bodies, full of energy and vision. There will never be a moment of boredom among His people on the New Earth.
>
> ➤ Deep in our hearts, we all desire a resurrected life on a resurrected Earth instead of a disembodied existence in a spiritual realm. <u>Why do we desire this?</u>
>
> ➤ We desire it because it is God's plan for us to be raised to a new life on the New Earth.
>
> ➤ It is our Lord who created us to desire what we were made for.
>
> **HE DESIGNED US TO LIVE ON EARTH AND TO DESIRE THE EARTHLY LIFE.**

Notes:
_____
_____
_____
_____

BREAK-TIME   **(Slides # 58 - 59)**

(Slides # 60 thru # 62)

LIFE ON THE NEW HEAVEN & NEW EARTH

The birth of Jesus Christ two thousand years ago brought heaven down to earth; not earth up to heaven.

The coming New Earth will be God's permanent dwelling place and will be as pure and holy as Heaven has ever been.

> **God's greatest gift to us is "Himself." His presence brings about great joy and is fully satisfying; while His absence brings thirst and longing.**
>
> ➤ One can easily see the joylessness in the unbelieving world. Joylessness is present even among the wealthiest people on earth.
>
> ➤ Kings, politicians, and celebrities who are worshipped by masses of followers are really empty and lonely in their private lives and therefore seek for personal joy in the world of sexual immorality, alcohol, drugs, and riches giving them power and control over others.
>
> ➤ Now, the Book of Ecclesiastics on the OT reveals these hearts of joylessness among the rich and powerful.
>
> ➤ **Nobody will ever find true joy until they seek the presence of the Lord, who will then, open His arms and embrace them.**

Notes:

Curiosity about heaven frequently surfaces as family and friends gather together to socialize.

Such questions as:

What will our bodies be like? Will we eat and drink on the New Earth? What will we know and learn? What will our daily lives be like? Will we desire relationship with our loved ones again as well as with God? ***Will animals inhabit the New Earth?*** *What about our pets? Will there be art, entertainment, and sports? Will we design new technology? What will be the mode of travel?* ***Will we explore the stars and planets in the universe?*** *Whom will we meet and what will we experience together? And Finally -* ***Will we be with our family and friends forever?***

The finest book that I have read which addresses these questions and many others is Randy Alcorn's book entitled "Heaven."

We will one day pass from this Earth to the present Heaven through death, but eventually we'll be back to live forever on the restored Earth.

➢ We are pilgrims in this life, not because our home will never be on Earth, but because our ultimate home isn't on the present Earth which is still under the Curse.

➢ It was always the plan of our Lord for physical human beings to live on a physical Earth.

When sin entered the world of mankind, our Lord didn't abandon His plan; instead, He chose to become a Man on this same Earth.

<u>Why?</u>
➢ So that His people would experience His glory forever and that the Lord Himself could enjoy the company of men and women in the world that He made for us.

Notes:
_____
_____
_____
_____
_____
_____
_____
_____
_____
_____

(Slides # 63 thru # 65)

"BEHOLD, I AM COMING SOON!"

> "And behold, I am coming soon. Blessed is the one who keeps the words of the prophecy of this book." **Revelation 22:7**
>
> "Behold, I am coming soon, bringing my recompense with me, to repay everyone for what he has done. **Revelation 22:12**
>
> He who testifies to these things says, "Surely I am coming soon." Amen. Come, Lord Jesus! **Revelation 22:20**

Jesus is coming soon and He has told us how He would come.

> - He would come accompanied by wars, plagues, famines, persecutions, sufferings, and in a generation when knowledge would greatly increase.
>
> - And as the appointed time of His coming draws closer, the more intense the power of His enemies will assert itself.
>
> - Yes, He is coming very soon, but to understand just how rapidly Jesus is coming, we need to consider what must take place before His actual physical coming.
>
> - Thus, the Book of Revelation was written not only to provide essential information for the last generation, but also to encourage the church in all generations to maintain their steadfast loyalty in the midst of demonic pressures and persecutions.
>
> - We may not know the exact timing of His return but it will be unexpected to many **for He comes as "a thief in the night."**

For His people who are not in darkness, but remain awake, His coming will not be unexpected as He tells us:

> For you yourselves are fully aware that the day of the Lord will come like a thief in the night. While people are saying, "There is peace and security," then sudden destruction will come upon them as labor pains come upon a pregnant woman, and they will not escape.
>
> But you are not in darkness, brothers, for that day to surprise you like a thief. For you are all children of light, children of the day. We are not of the night or of the darkness. So then let us not sleep, as others do, but let us keep awake and be sober. **1 Thessalonians 5:1-6**

- **There are many followers of Christ today who are awake and like the "Sons of Issachar" – they are discerning that the time of His coming lies shortly before us; most probably in this generation.**

(Slides # 66 & 67)

THE BOOK OF REVELATION MUST REMAIN OPEN TO BOTH - THE KINGDOM OF GOD & THE KINGDOM OF THIS WORLD

When this Book is opened and expounded, it will strengthen the faith and hope of the people of God. However, it will also bring much ridicule from both within and outside the church:

- There will be many who will have nothing to do with it; they will mock and belittle those who proclaim it. They will say, "You are a dreaming, hateful pessimist who is scaring people."

- Even among evangelical Christians, there are those who will have nothing to do with it. They like to say "don't worry about it for things will all "pan-out" in the end."

- This is a very dangerous mindset that may lead one to being among the five virgins who were unprepared for His coming and reacted too late to enter into the marriage feast with Jesus. It wasn't their unbelief in Christ that kept them out; it was their apathetic attitude toward preparedness for His coming.

- This Book of Revelation will also arouse opposition among the unbelievers whose hope lies only in the future of this present world; for this prophetic book leaves no hope for their vain dreams for they desire to establish a united worldly government.

- **Those who proclaim these end-time prophecies will one day be considered a threat to the national security of our country.**

What then? Should we keep the Book closed because of a threatening and hateful opposition? <u>**No!**</u> **Because we are to:**

> Let the evildoer still do evil, and the filthy still be filthy, and the righteous still do right, and the holy still be holy." **Revelation 22:11**

This Book will draw the lines.

- It will strengthen and emphasize the great difference between the true people of God and those of the world.

- It will make the people of the world more conscious of the great difference between their worldly desires and those of the people of God;

- It will also make God's people more conscious of the great difference between their desires and the worldly desires.

- And for this latter reason, the Book must not remain closed, but must be open so that all can hear and read and this two-fold effect may be achieved.

Stand fast Christian warriors; the truths in this prophetic Book need to be openly proclaimed to this generation of both believers as well as non-believers.

A FINAL WARNING

> I warn everyone who hears the words of the prophecy of this book: if anyone adds to them, God will add to him the plagues described in this book, and if anyone takes away from the words of the book of this prophecy, God will take away his share in the tree of life and in the holy city, which are described in this book. **Revelation 22:18-19**

Now, the warning in these verses does not apply to the imperfect understanding of believers who read and teach this Book. After all, these words are prophetic and therefore, there are inherent difficulties in its interpretation.

No, this "warning" does not refer to misunderstanding the Book, but it refers to a deliberate attitude of unbelieving what is recorded in this Book.

- ➢ It is addressed to those who are acquainted with its contents but would change the message of this Book to suit their own purposes, so that the Kingdom of the World is confused with the Kingdom of God.

- ➢ They do it by adding or detracting from it, so that the light of the truth of this prophecy is dimmed.

- ➢ For example, they deny the truth of a physical coming of Jesus Christ by "spiritualizing" these scriptures - or by denying the "inerrancy" of these truths.

- ➢ Those who do this must be aware of the punishment that awaits; that is, they could very well be deprived of their part in the Book of Life.

Notes:

(Slides # 69 thru # 71)

SEVEN BEATITUDES IN THE BOOK OF REVELATION

Blessed is the one who reads aloud the words of this prophecy, and blessed are those who hear, and who keep what is written in it, for the time is near. **Revelation 1:3**

Blessed are the dead who die in the Lord from now on." "Blessed indeed," says the Spirit, "that they may rest from their labors, for their deeds follow them!" **Revelation 14:13**

"Behold, I am coming like a thief! Blessed is the one who stays awake, keeping his garments on, that he may not go about naked and be seen exposed!" **Revelation 16:15**

Blessed are those who are invited to the marriage supper of the Lamb." **Revelation 19:9**

Blessed and holy is the one who shares in the first resurrection! Over such the second death has no power, but they will be priests of God and of Christ, and they will reign with him for a thousand years. **Revelation 20:6**

"And behold, I am coming soon. Blessed is the one who keeps the words of the prophecy of this book." **Revelation 22:7**

Blessed are those who wash their robes, so that they may have the right to the tree of life and that they may enter the city by the gates. **Revelation 22:14**

"The grace of our Lord Jesus Christ be with you all. Amen"

Additional Notes:

THE LAMB OF GOD - OUR TRUE "COMMANDER-IN-CHIEF"

The days are rapidly approaching when a tremendous separation will take place among mankind.

Yet, during this present era of warfare, He reigns as our Commander-in-Chief and His Name continues to be the battle cry for those warriors who fight daily for righteousness and truth.

His name is Jesus, Our Lord, Our King, Our Commander-in-Chief

➢ A truly mighty Leader who would never delegate assignments to His people that He Himself wouldn't readily embrace.

➢ A Commander that Christian warriors will readily follow not matter the danger or what costs have to be paid.

➢ These are warriors whose deepest desire is to hear Jesus welcome them with the following words when they enter into His presence:

.... 'Well done, good and faithful servant. You have been faithful over a little; I will set you over much. Enter into the joy of your master.' *Matthew 25:21*

CHRISTIAN WARRIORS
IT'S TIME TO "RISE-UP"

SESSION #15 – WORKBOOK
Intended For
"KINGDOM WARRIORS IN THE ARMY OF GOD"

Unveiling Mysteries in the "Book of Revelation"

Based upon the Book:
GOD'S ANOINTED WARRIORS
By
Dr. Donald Bell
Major USMC, Ret.

(Slides # 2 - 3)

CALLING WARRIOR-SPIRITED CHRISTIANS TO "RISE-UP"

The purpose for this session is to prepare soldiers in the army of God for the coming battles by providing some preparation ideas for Warrior-Spirited Christians to "Rise Up' and lead others through the extremely challenging tribulation events - that are soon coming upon America, as well as the entire world.

➢ Yes, this will be a period of great trouble, even greater than that flood that took place in the days of Noah, for this will be a time of horrendous worldwide suffering which will affect billions of people around the world.

(Slides # 4 thru 6)

WARRIOR–SPIRITED CHRISTIANS ------ WHO ARE THEY?

They are men and women within a remnant of Christianity, who possess a deep, passionate heart commitment for our Lord. Warriors are acknowledged as those who are determined to do battle for their beloved King and His Kingdom.

➢ These are Christians who will "NEVER RETREAT" from their calling, no matter the circumstances. They are more committed to their "King" than they are to their own lives.

➢ They have hearts that will never compromise their faith in Jesus Christ - even if it leads to persecution and martyrdom.

The heart of a Warrior-Spirited Christian embraces the following callings of Jesus ---that is, they have a deep desire:

➢ To be numbered among the remnant of God's people who live a life that labels us as "Overcomers" in Revelation 2 & 3.

➢ To live out the Christian attributes found in the Beatitudes of Jesus in Matthew 5 & 6.

➢ To be numbered among the "five virgins" who maintain oil in their lamps while awaiting the Lord's coming in Matthew 25.

➢ To live out our daily lives with a deep desire to hear the Lord Jesus say to us, "Well done, good and faithful servant" when we enter into His presence. (Matthew 25:21)

(Slide # 7)

A SPIRITUAL WAR

Warrior-Spirited Christians in the Army of God must recognize that we are up against an enemy who is incredibly powerful; one whom the great majority of the world's population fails to recognize and thus, they are enslaved to that spiritual darkness.

Scriptures reveal that there is a violent, ongoing war raging in the spiritual realm - in which the people of God must actively participate.

> **It is a war** - "not directed against flesh and blood, but against the rulers, against the authorities, against the powers of this dark world, and against the spiritual forces of evil in the heavenly realms" **Ephesians 6:12**

Both the light and the darkness are coming to full maturity in these times and thus, evil is mobilizing for the battle against the forces of light.

➢ This is becoming more and more visible in America as the dark, demonically controlled, leftist governments will soon launch their hatred of Almighty God against His church.

(Slide # 8)

RECOGNIZE THESE TRUTHS:

1. This world is in iniquity and will fight to the last against Jesus Christ and His Kingdom on this earth.

2. The heavenly Kingdom of God will come only after world-wide tribulation events - evolving in the persecution of His church which will separate the true Christians from the false.

3. There is an apostate part of the church that will compromise and align itself with the world leading to the betrayal of other Christians.

4. It is through times of tribulation that true righteousness is clearly manifested. For the weeds which were sown among thorns will be separated from the good seeds that have been sown on fertile soil.

(Slides # 9 thru 14)

CALLING FOR LEADERS IN THE ARMY OF GOD

Every Christian in the Army of God has the potential to positively impact other people for the Kingdom of God. Those who know that they are called to minister to others are also called to be **leaders**.

- ➢ Their ministry may be teaching, discipling, pastoring, evangelizing, intercessory prayer warriors, or assisting those who do these things.
- ➢ These are all leadership positions in the Army of God and those who are called to these various ministries are also called to pursue -----
  - ➢ "GREATNESS IN LEADERSHIP."

Greatness In Leadership Is Not An Attribute One Is Born With; It Must Be Earned. Greatness Is Not Pursued For The Sake Of Greatness.

- ➢ It is about one's desire to die to himself, his ambitions, and his personal comforts in order to achieve his calling in life.

- ➢ Jesus Christ, our Commander in Chief has a predestined mission for each of His people, and those who actively seek for it will find it; and those who find it must then act upon it.

- ➢ Such actions will produce Great Leaders who can impact many lives for the kingdom of God.

- ➢ Such leaders have a deep passion to see the kingdom of God manifested in glorious strength, not simply in the institutional churches, but in the workplaces, the neighborhoods, the downtown areas, and individual homes, where "real life" occurs.

Warrior-spirited leaders also recognize that they have weaknesses, but the difference is that they are committed to focusing on their strengths.

- ➢ This creates a spirit of excitement when there is no expectation to continue in one's weaker, less gifted areas.

- ➢ They trust their fellow leaders to provide fruit in those areas where they are less gifted.

- ➢ Thus, great leaders have no desire to control everything, for their sole focus is on God and His kingdom people.

> **Finally, warrior-spirited leadership has little to do with rank and everything to do with responsibility. Leaders think, envision, and ask questions, but above all, these leaders "<u>act</u>."**
>
> ➤ Even when leaders don't think they are capable, when they realize they are weak and fear begins to invade their consciousness, they still step up to the plate and "**act**" like leaders.
>
> **Where does one go to get these leadership attributes?**
>
> ➤ One must first die to himself, his worldly ambitions and his fleshly desires, so that he may understand & pursue the Lord's calling & to live for others who are seeking direction for their lives.

<u>**Listen to Paul - a warrior-spirited leader as he speaks to his followers:**</u>

> Be watchful, stand firm in the faith, <u>act like men</u>, be strong. Let all that you do be done in love.
> 1 Corinthians 16:13-14

So keep yourself on the pathway that leads upward. Stay close to our truly greatest Leader, Jesus Christ, and He will make you a warrior-spirited leader that many others will gladly follow.

A MILITARY PERSPECTIVE OF A GREAT LEADER

> A leader does not abide in his tent while his men bleed and die upon the battlefield. A leader does not dine while his men go hungry or sleep when they stand at watch upon the wall. A leader does not command his men's loyalty through fear or purchase it with gold; he earns their love by the sweat of his own back and the pains he endures for their sake. That which comprises the harshest burden, a leader lifts first and sets down last. A leader does not require service of those he leads; he provides it to them. He serves them, not they him.[52]

These certainly are the leadership traits inherent within the greatest Leader that ever walked on this earth and who currently serves as the true Commander in Chief over the Army of God.

<u>Notes</u> - Consider your personal calling to leadership in the Kingdom of God- Can you hear it?

_____
_____
_____
_____
_____

---

[52] Greg Austin, Pastor & Vietnam Veteran

(Slides # 15 thru 18)

SELF-DISCIPLINE IN LEADERSHIP

A priority of great leadership is <u>self-discipline</u> in day-to-day living.

- ➢ Warrior-spirited leaders need discipline at those times of the day when they are at their weakest, those times when the spirit of procrastination invariably falls upon them.

- ➢ Warrior-spirited leaders need to learn through growing experiences to deal with such issues and not allow worldly temptations to render them impotent during this time.

- ➢ If we do not conquer such temptations, we become POWs in the camp of the enemy for a short period of time. And at some point, it becomes recognizable, for it creates a deep emptiness in our spirit and a sense of depression begins to creep into out soul.

- ➢ Warrior-spirited leaders must learn that walking as disciples of Jesus means "redeeming the time" throughout each day for Him.

Sadly, the vast majority of American Christians spend the bulk of their days in these POW camps.
- ➢ Among these are many who may have been called to a leadership role, yet did not forsake their lives and thus did not achieve their full calling.

- ➢ They are certainly among the saints of God, but they did not attain to the leadership role to which God had called them.

Every one of us faces these temptations toward apathy, as <u>it is an ongoing attack from the enemy.</u>
- ➢ Today, we must continually resist worldly temptations and prepare to "be ready" for the Day of the Lord lies shortly before us.

- ➢ Warrior leadership in the Army of God in these last days must be totally committed to walk the pathway that the Lord Jesus Christ, our true Commander-in-Chief, has laid before them.

One further note of caution:

Christian soldiers are more susceptible to attacks from the enemy immediately following a significant spiritual victory.

- ➢ This is a principle that military leaders learn during combat—we are more vulnerable to enemy counterattack immediately after achieving a hard-fought objective.

- ➢ As we begin to internally celebrate our victory, we have a tendency to relax and let down our guard. Be careful here, for this is the most critical time for a counterattack by our enemy.

(Slides # 19 thru 21)

WARRIORS ON THE BATTLEFIELD OF LIFE

> **God's Army May Not Be Large, But There Has Never Been One More Powerful.**
>
> ➤ They refuse to retreat before the enemies of the Cross and their faithfulness that may even lead to death is far more powerful than death itself.
>
> ➤ Soldiers in the army of God are not fearful of dying because they have already died to the things of this world and now, they live to do all things for the sake of the gospel because of their deep love for the Lord.
>
> ➤ Mighty warriors of God would never run from the sound of a battle for they know that there cannot be victory without a battle.
>
> **Warrior leadership in the Army of God in these last days must be totally committed to walk the pathway that the Lord Jesus Christ has laid before them.**

Soldiers in His army must take up the Cross daily, not occasionally.

> For the word of the cross is foolishness to those who are perishing, but to us who are being saved it is the power of God. *1 Corinthians 1:18*

Our life focus is to seek the will of the Lord, not our own will for we are called to become a living sacrifice.

> I appeal to you therefore, brothers, by the mercies of God, to present your bodies as a living sacrifice, holy and acceptable to God, which is your spiritual worship. Do not be conformed to this world, but be transformed by the renewal of your mind, that by testing you may discern what is the will of God, what is good and acceptable and perfect. **Romans 12:1-2**

We need to let go of worldly ways and embrace our calling into the Kingdom of God.

BREAK-TIME **(Slides # 22 - 23)**

(Slide # 24)

SEEKING OUR MISSION IN THE ARMY OF GOD

As warrior leadership in the Army of God in these last days, we must be totally committed to walk the pathway that Jesus Christ, our Commander in Chief has laid before each of us.

> The following is an example of a **_general mission calling_** that is designed to drive Christian leadership through the wilderness journey of a committed life to the Lord.
>
> Each of us should memorize this "**_general mission calling_**" and pray daily that it will be carried out in each of our lives.
>
> ➢ *Day by day, to live out the spirit of the gospel in my life in such a way that it will positively affect others for the strengthening and expanding of the kingdom of God and to stand strong for my Lord Jesus Christ against the forces of darkness in this world.*

> **Now, as we continually seek His calling on our lives He will reveal to each of us our _specific mission_ to which we are called.**
>
> ➢ This **_specific mission_** resides in the passion of our individual hearts, and our direction toward fulfilling this calling becomes clearer as it is written down and prayed for each day.
>
> ➢ Therefore, it is important for each of us to internalize our personal understanding of our individual mission(s) to which He has called us.

> **The church is about to enter a very challenging time, which is also a necessary prerequisite for entry into its most fruitful times. The darkness is gathering its forces, but so is the light.**
>
> ➢ The Lord has given each of us a specific part to play in His overall plan, and it must be our continual quest to search for our individual mission assignment.
>
> ➢ Almost everyone has a vision for what they want to accomplish, but it's going to require a difficult and continuous work discipline.

Record your calling to specific mission(s):

_____
_____
_____
_____
_____

(Slides # 25 - 26)

OUR MISSIONAL CALLING

When we look at the cities of the United States, many of us envision Christians as a people going about their daily business with little sense of their personal calling. Certainly, they all look forward to one day entering into the eternal presence of the Lord, but will they hear our Lord Jesus say, on that day when they enter into His presence,

> *Well done, good and faithful servant. You have been faithful over a little; I will set you over much. Enter into the joy of your master. (**Matthew 25:21**)*

Key Points:

Perhaps not every Christian who enters into His presence will hear those words. Now this isn't speaking about our salvation - **each of us has a mission assigned that we must pursue; and in order to hear those words, we must move forward in the Lord and His mission for us.**

This doesn't mean simply being faithful in church attendance and tithing. That is all well and good, but each of us has his or her own mission. **Don't ignore it - Seek for it!**

> - **Wherever you work, you have a mission—seek for it!**
> - **Wherever you live, you have a mission—seek for it!**

We are all called to be partakers of the work God intends to complete, which will usher in the reign of our Lord on this earth.

> - If we don't complete our assigned mission, someone else will, and then that person will reap the reward that was initially set aside for us.

Remember this, there can be no victory without entering into the battle – we must see every challenge that comes into our lives as a great opportunity to fulfill our calling to leadership in the Kingdom of God.

Notes - Record your mission calling at work & home:

_____
_____
_____
_____
_____
_____
_____

(Slides # 27 - 28)

THE FRONTLINES OF THE SPIRITUAL BATTLEFIELD

Christians need to awaken to the realization that the traditional church is not where the majority of the Lord's soldiers are expected to carry on their respective ministerial assignments.

➢ Now, for those in pastoral ministry, their respective churches are certainly the frontlines of their spiritual battlefield.

➢ But for the majority of Christians, the mission of the traditional church is in the rear, with the responsibility of equipping the troops in the army of God to be sent to the respective frontlines of the spiritual battlefield.

Key Points:

There is a growing need for Christians to arise and minister to those people who will not be found in Sunday church services.

Now Christian soldiers may ask, "<u>Where are the frontlines of our respective battlefields?</u>"

<u>**Well, ask yourself the following questions:**</u>

➢ Where is that place outside of our homes and churches, where Christian soldiers can have a tremendous impact for the kingdom of God?

➢ Where is that place that requires so much of our time and effort in life and yet, most of us approach it grudgingly?

➢ Where is that place where the Lord brings so many people into our lives over the years and yet, most do not envision it as a ministry opportunity?

Notes:
_____
_____
_____
_____
_____
_____
_____

(Slides # 29 - 30)

MINISTERING IN THE WORKPLACE

Early Christians made the workplace their ministerial focus because their occupations regularly took them there. As a result, the workplace played a vital role in establishing and expanding the early church.

➢ In fact, most early followers of Jesus remained in full-time business while simultaneously conducting full-time ministry.

Key Points:

Christian soldiers need to realize that today millions of God's people are similarly called to full-time ministry in their respective business occupations.

➢ It makes no difference what your occupation is - <u>all can have great influence in their respective areas of employment, for that is where they encounter the world and that is where their lives have been positioned by the Lord.</u>

Contrary to what many traditional churches imply, there is no hierarchal distinction between pastors and ordinary people in the eyes of our Lord.

➢ The calling to pastoral ministry is not necessarily higher than the blue-collar workers driving daily through rush-hour traffic to get to work in order to provide a living for their families.

➢ Christians who work in jobs outside the confines of the church need to understand that they are not perpetual privates in God's army just because they have not gone to seminary.

➢ They need to discover that they have the potential to become full-fledged "generals" whose ministry influence can grow far beyond the bounds of the workplace and the walls of their local church and into the very heart of the city.

Unfortunately, many of these workplace ministers fail to fulfill their divine destiny because they are often derided by others as untrained or uneducated.

➢ This is not a new accusation. Both Peter and John, who were fishermen by profession, certainly experienced this ridiculing.
➢ Additionally, Jesus, who was a carpenter, recruited His disciples from the workplace rather than from those who were trained in the synagogues.

Notes:

_____
_____
_____
_____

(Slide # 31)

A GREAT MAJORITY OF MEN REFUSE TO GO TO CHURCH

Many workingmen refuse to identify with the pastoral culture in today's churches and therefore will not seek help from the church.

➤ Yet, deep within themselves, many of these folks, who may be your fellow employees, or customers, unknowingly hunger for strong Christian with whom they can relate; namely, peers who understand their world and their ongoing temptations and struggles.

➤ Those who have lost loved ones through death, divorce, or adultery are unknowingly searching for someone who may be able to restore some degree of comfort to their lives.

➤ There are many people on this battlefield of life who hopelessly see themselves in dead-end jobs: young men paying fifty percent of their paycheck for child support; blue-collar workers hanging out in casinos, hoping to change their status in life; and small business owners struggling to stay afloat.

This provides a tremendous opportunity for Christ's anointed warriors to move toward the front of this battlefield to fight for the souls of their fellow workers.

➤ Great missional opportunities present themselves in the workplace on a daily basis, yet a warrior for Christ must take the initiative, or opportunities will be lost.

➤ Soldiers become warrior leaders when they commit to making personal sacrifices in order to show a true, loving concern for those people encountered daily in the workplace.

(Slide # 32)

Our Overall Assigned Mission Is To Lead Those Held In Captivity By The World

➤ Out of the darkness of this world & into the light of the Lord's kingdom

➤ From the deception of this world unto the truth found in the Lord's kingdom

➤ From the evilness of this world into the righteousness of the Lord's kingdom

➤ From eternal damnation and misery into eternal life and joy in the Lord's kingdom

Christians become warrior-spirited leaders when they commit to making personal sacrifices in order to show a true, loving concern for those people encountered daily in the workplace.

(Slides # 33 - 34)

As one ministering in the business world, I have written a letter that I send annually to several hundred of my clients.

> **Friendships and trust were built with my client base over several years, and this letter, which communicates a loving concern for them, continues to open several doors for ministry opportunities.**
>
> - A copy of this letter entitled "An Urgent Message for Truly Valued Friends" is available in Appendix "E" of my book entitled "God's Anointed Warriors."
>
> - Perhaps it will help you draft a letter communicating your burden for family members, fellow employees, neighbors, or others.
>
> - At any rate, it's a way to introduce yourself as a Christian
>
> **Some may respond and others may ignore your letter BUT when sudden catastrophic events strike our nation, many of those who have ignored it will certainly run to you for understanding of what is taking place as well as for your leadership direction.**

> **Christian Warriors, this is a critical time to sound the alarm. Many of our fellow workers, though not Christians, are very concerned about events that are taking place in our country.**
>
> - Taking advantage of opportunities to speak with them concerning today's economic concerns, potential terrorist activity, and increased violence throughout the country definitely will open up most people to serious conversation.
>
> - Once they realize your concern for them, communication becomes more frequent and open, and then it is only a small step to speak of the warnings given in Scripture and the call of Jesus Christ on their lives.

Notes:

_____
_____
_____
_____
_____
_____
_____

BREAK-TIME   **(Slides # 35 - 36)**

(Slides #38 - 39)

COMING TO AMERICA – GOD'S RIGHTEOUS JUDGMENT

The United States as a democratic nation is rapidly disappearing – constitutional law will soon be ignored. As Christians, we cannot put our trust in financial institutions or government promises. **All this is of the world and God's people need to come out of the world.**

> **Those of us who correctly discern the times recognize that God's righteous judgment will soon descend upon America.**
>
> <u>What type of Judgment?</u>
> - There have been numerous times in the history of the world when our Lord rained down judgments from heaven. Such as: earthquakes, plagues, hurricanes, tornados, etc.
>
> - However, throughout history our Lord has also chosen to stir up the hearts of nations ruled by evil governments to launch attacks upon a nation that has historically known Him, but have fallen into immorality and left Him to pursue their own sinful pleasures.

> <u>Think about these scenarios:</u>
> - A sudden economic collapse much like the 1929 stock market crash that occurred overnight resulting in sudden bank closures, multiple suicides, famine, diseases, families being thrown out of their homes. All this launched the great depression of the 1930's.
>
> - Multiple nuclear terrorist strikes that will suddenly hit many cities (probably coastal) in our nation and before ordinary folks like us can adjust; the grocery stores, banks, and gas stations will be locked down. It is quite possible that this may happen in the midst of a Middle Eastern war which will affect the entire world.
>
> - It is also possible that because of our open borders policy, terrorists of today could be smuggling nuclear suitcase bombs into numerous American cities and coordinating for a devastating attack upon our nation.
>
> - Consider what American life would look like a few seconds after an EMP (electromagnetic pulse) incident - a nuclear weapon detonated high above the center of the United States. This would result in a large number of automobiles, airplanes, computers, cellular networks, home electricity, etc throughout our nation being immediately rendered useless for years.

Whatever the scenario, it will certainly be a series of "sudden" catastrophic events unforeseen by the great majority in this country.

Notes:
_____
_____
_____

(Slides # 40 thru 43)

COMING TO AMERICA – GOD'S RIGHTEOUS JUDGMENT

Such catastrophic events will launch more devastation than a thousand 9-11's.

> **Resulting in:**
> ➤ Great panic as people swarm to the banks, the grocery stores, the gas stations. They will not have a "customer mentality" – but a panicky, uncontrollable mob with no direction other than to grab and run with no concern for who gets hurt.
>
> **Immediate after-effects:**
> ➤ Neighbors beating on neighbors' doors seeking food. Stone throwing – breaking windows. Caring not for who gets hurt.
> ➤ Subsequently, after scourging the urban areas, youth gangs will form and go out to the suburban areas. Their intent is to intimidate families, burglarize homes, and murder those who oppose them.
>
> **Governmental Response:**
> ➤ Government militia forces will eventually unite to bring their "version of order" to the urban areas. Historical events in other countries tell us that eventually, such militia forces will attempt to confiscate all firearms as well as the storage of foods and supplies.

This time of tremendous challenge is rapidly approaching and in the near future, we will need to stand "shoulder to shoulder" with one another and work together in developing our personal missions focusing upon how we will move forward from here.

> **Those who understand the chaotic challenges that will soon confront our generation need to be communicating with their families and friends.**
> ➤ The purpose for this communication is to address "physical preparations" that will needed in the event of a sudden shutdown of banks, stores, gas stations, and subsequent gang violence throughout cities and neighborhoods.

> **Gather together in a small group, perhaps 7 or 8 of your close friends and family members who are like-minded concerning the approaching chaos. Then discuss in detail the following ideas for preparedness:**
>
> 1. Discuss food supplies for a minimum of six to twelve months.
> 2. Discuss drinking and cleansing water for an indefinite period of time.
> 3. Discuss medical supplies, batteries, toilet paper, gasoline, propane, tools, flashlights, radios.
> 4. Discuss supplies needed to survive a lengthy, cold winter without electrical power.
> 5. Discuss prepared supplies that may be a blessing - to your unprepared neighbors.
> 6. Discuss the probability of gang violence in your community.
> 7. Discuss the ownership and use of firearms in a volatile situation.
> 8. Finally, discuss the relationship that each individual member of the gathered families and friends - has with the Lord- and develop a plan of how to proceed with the deepening of each relationship.
>
> **More specific information concerning this preparation overview is provided in Appendix G of my book entitled "God's Anointed Warriors."**

(Slide # 44 thru 48)

COMING TO AMERICA – PERSECUTION OF CHRISTIANS

A generation of American Christians is watching the early birth pains convinced by their teachers that the next major event will be the rapture of the church or a sudden, peaceful return of Christ; <u>yet what is actually before us is intense persecution.</u>

These are Christians in America who completely miss the point that the Lord makes in the following passage regarding events at the end of the age:

> "Then they will deliver you up to tribulation and put you to death, and you will be hated by all nations for my name's sake. And then many will fall away and betray one another and hate one another. And many false prophets will arise and lead many astray. And because lawlessness will be increased, the love of many will grow cold. But the one who endures to the end will be saved. And this gospel of the kingdom will be proclaimed throughout the whole world as a testimony to all nations, **and then the end will come**. *Matthew 24:9-14*

This will happen in America!

- What other country has such a large Christian population that will "fall away" at the end of the age?
- However, most Americans are neither emotionally nor spiritually prepared for the sudden and intense persecution that is shortly before us.
- Nominal professing Christians will stumble and fall under the threat of persecution and will deny their faith.
- They will also betray those who were once their friends who continue to stand strong in the Lord.

Also, other American churches that embrace the visions of their forerunners in Sardis and Laodicea will unite against the true believers in the Lord Jesus Christ.

- These are led by false teachers who will eagerly embrace the universal doctrines of religion that are acceptable to the kingdom of the world.

- These are beliefs that will mock those who proclaim that Jesus Christ is the eternal Son of God and the only way to eternal life.

- They will join with the Babylonian whore on top of the seven-headed beast in order to continue sharing in her riches and beauty and retain their popular position in American society.

- These are the **weeds** among the **good seeds** that may deny the blood of our Lord Jesus, but have an unquenchable lust for the blood of His martyrs. <u>They are a part of the religious nature of Mystery Babylon.</u>[53]

---
[53] Matthew 13:24-26

For the American believer, it is hard to imagine that Christian persecution could happen in our country, much less begin to prepare for it.

> - It may be even more severe in America than in other nations; for here is where the enemy will concentrate his efforts to stamp out the name of Christ from the Christian church.
>
> - Read **Romans 1:18-31** to see what happens to mankind when they trade the truths of God for lies. **This is America in scripture**

Realize this:

This persecution of steadfast Christians will be foundational for the coming move of God, a terrifying and glorious revival that will bring the true Gospel of Christ to the forefront of humanity.

- Thus, this period of tribulation will produce a final harvest of souls and a revival that awakens many sincere Christians who have been put to sleep by their teachers.

- The leaders of this movement will have paid the price, like the first disciples, who stood up and challenged the falseness that had infiltrated the true church.

- These Christian leaders will guard the sheep and speak forth in the power of God. There is a showdown coming between true Christian leadership and the false.

Notes – Consider how you, your family, & friends will handle persecution from government and worldly churches:

_____
_____
_____
_____
_____
_____
_____
_____
_____
_____
_____
_____
_____
_____

BREAK-TIME　　　　　　　　　　　　　　　　**(Slides # 49 - 50)**

(Slide # 12)

CHRISTIAN WARRIORS ENDURING HARDSHIPS

In the coming days, true believers in Jesus Christ will be challenged from every direction. Every believer who commits to an all-out relationship with our Lord will come under spiritual oppression, various afflictions, and persecution.

- We may initially struggle in our trials because discipline and suffering is foreign to us, but as we continue to endure, we will recognize how meaningful the discipline of the Lord really is.

- Our hearts will continually grow deeper in our love and commitment to Him. At times it may seem unbearable when some friends and even family members become spiteful toward us.

Enduring the scorn and persecution from the world joins us in a partnership with Christ as we share in His sufferings in this life.

- Suffering with Christ produces a strong heart bond in our relationship with Him and with one another as we follow Him down the same path that He walked.

- For a deep spiritual love for one another begins to grow which will throw off all the cares of this world and focus only upon the Kingdom of God in this world.

In order to better comprehend this, consider the following: Marines in combat or boot camp who experience really tough trials together eventually grow in strength and closeness with one another. Marines will put their own lives on the line for their fellow Marines.

- Yet a heart that experiences the hardships that Christ also experienced produces a much greater bond than what Marines share with each other.

Listen to Paul encouraging Christians to endure persecution:

> Share in suffering as a good soldier of Christ Jesus. No soldier gets entangled in civilian pursuits, since his aim is to please the one who enlisted him. *2 Timothy 2:3-4*

> We are afflicted in every way, but not crushed; perplexed, but not driven to despair; persecuted, but not forsaken; struck down, but not destroyed; always carrying in the body the death of Jesus, so that the life of Jesus may also be manifested in our bodies. For we who live are always being given over to death for Jesus' sake, so that the life of Jesus also may be manifested in our mortal flesh. So death is at work in us, but life in you. **2 Corinthians 4:8-12**

> So we do not lose heart. Though our outer nature is wasting away, our inner nature is being renewed day by day. For this slight momentary affliction is preparing for us an eternal weight of glory beyond all comparison, as we look not to the things that are seen but to the things that are unseen. For the things that are seen are transient, but the things that are unseen are eternal. **2 Corinthians 4:16-18**

My dear brothers & sisters of our Lord – We are called to Endure suffering! For we are soldiers in the Army of God.
- **In other words: "Endure suffering son! You are a soldier in the Lord's army. You have been trained to undergo hardship on the spiritual battlefield."**

Notes:

(Slides # 55 - 56)

EVIL DISGUISED AS DECENCY – "STAND FAST"

Key Points:

Evil disguised as decency in the midst of a lukewarm Christian community, may be strong weapons the enemy will use against you.

➢ These are pacifists that will attack your faith and attempt to get you to make compromises so that life won't be so hard. **Stand fast!**

During these times of persecution, the voice of Satan will undoubtedly attack many with, "this is too hard…..it's not fair….God has forsaken me."

➢ Be aware that when these thoughts begin to surface that you are a soldier in the Army of God under attack. **Stand fast!**

➢ This will be tough when loved ones embrace you and try to get you to compromise your faith just a little bit by saying, "Daddy please, God will understand." **Stand fast!**

Your steadfastness is of tremendous importance to both you and your loved ones who are considering small compromises.

➢ It will have a powerful strengthening effect on all who see your uncompromising testimony which prioritizes the Kingdom of God over the world.

Your family and friends may grieve over your steadfastness that leads to persecution, but they too will be strengthened in their lives as they witness your steadfast commitment to the Lord. For they will see you as a Great Leader as well as a disciple of our Greatest Leader – Jesus Christ.

Notes:

(Slides # 57 thru 61)

HANDLING SUFFERING IN THE ARMY OF GOD

The Lord's word tells us that suffering is a necessary experience that His warriors must endure in order to receive His glory. Being "prepared" doesn't mean we won't suffer.

> The Spirit himself bears witness with our spirit that we are children of God, and if children, then heirs — heirs of God and fellow heirs with Christ, provided we suffer with him in order that we may also be glorified with him. (**Romans 8:16-17**)

<u>One might ask, "What actually is suffering?"</u>

➢ Well, suffering may be physical, or it may be mental or emotional, but suffering really is anything that we don't like; anything that is uncomfortable or painful for us.

➢ Certainly the most painful suffering that may occur would be the loss of our loved ones, but our heavenly Father understands this, for He also experienced the loss of His Son.

➢ Our hope in such a grievous situation derives from understanding that - as the Father raised His Son from the dead that our loved ones who die in Christ will also be raised to eternal life with Him.

<u>Key Points:</u>

In the coming days, every believer who commits to an all-out relationship with our Lord will come under spiritual oppression, various afflictions, and persecution.

➢ We may initially struggle in our trials because discipline and suffering is foreign to us, but as we continue to endure, we will recognize how meaningful the discipline of the Lord really is.

➢ Our hearts will continually grow deeper in our love and commitment to Him.

Enduring the scorn and persecution from the world joins us in a partnership with Christ as we share in His sufferings in this life.

➢ It is through suffering in life that warrior-spirited leadership develops the characteristics of holiness that are inherent in His glory and allow them to become more and more conformed to the image of His Son.

➢ Sufferings in life should no longer be a surprise, yet leaders must learn to handle them today so we will be prepared tomorrow, when the trumpets begin to blast.

> **1 Peter 2:21-22**
> - ... *when you do good and **suffer** for it you endure, this is a gracious thing in the sight of God. For to this you have been called, because **Christ also suffered for you**, leaving you an example, so that you might follow in his steps.*
>
> - *He committed no sin, neither was deceit found in his mouth. When he was reviled, he did not revile in return; **when he suffered**, he did not threaten, but continued entrusting himself to him who judges justly.*

We must stand as warriors for Jesus Christ in the midst of good times and bad times; for both will be faced in life.

Think about how you will handle Suffering & Fear – be specific:

___
___
___
___
___
___
___
___
___
___
___
___
___
___
___
___
___
___
___
___
___
___
___
___

(Slides # 62 thru 64)

OVERCOMING "FEAR"

> **Fear** has the tendency to cause people to stick their heads in the sand and hope this won't happen.
>
> **Fear** will keep us from properly preparing and that day of tremendous warfare will then drop on us like a thief in the night.
>
> Our generation is going to face some very challenging times and more and more Christian warriors are needed for a tough battlefield that will bring forth a great multitude of people that will give their lives over to the Lord.
>
> ➢ People who will be searching for men and women of great spiritual strength in the midst of tremendous tribulations - those who are **not fearful** during these times.

I have learned from my experiences during the Vietnam War that the key to overcoming fear in warfare is by prioritizing the men under your authority over your own life.

> Key Points:
>
> **Now think about your loved ones in the midst of times when needed supplies will no longer be available and it will free you to make appropriate decisions concerning preparations.**
>
> ➢ This is not the time for God's people to withdraw into passivity – <u>Prioritize your family & friends before you and "fear" will no longer be in control of your decisions.</u>
>
> **Satan's worldly peoples will always visibly appear to be greater and more powerful than God's mighty warriors for they are usually in positions of worldly authority.**
>
> ➢ Yet, warrior-spirited Christians standing uncompromisingly for our Lord will always prevail in the strength of the Lord.
>
> ➢ The praying believer will never faint during hard times. On the contrary, he will grow stronger and stronger – because he trusts in God before he trusts in men.

> *He gives power to the faint, and to him who has no might he increases strength. Even youths shall faint and be weary, and young men shall fall exhausted; but they who **wait** for the Lord shall renew their strength; they shall mount up with wings like eagles; they shall run and not be weary; they shall walk and not faint. **(Isaiah 40:29-31)***

(Slides # 65 - 66)

COMBATING CONFUSION

Confusion Is One Of The Most Dominating Factors In Combat - That Brings About Defeat.

> **Great leadership will step up and take the initiative to be decisive in the midst of confusion.**
>
> ➢ Because confusion and uncertainty is so commonplace in the world, those with confidence in the direction they are going will inspire others.
>
> ➢ **Thus, courageous leadership is a necessary element to achieve victory over confusion for it also encourages others. Courage is a basic foundation for great leadership.**

COURAGE WILL DEFEAT "CONFUSION!"   COURAGE OVERCOMES "FEAR!"

> **Great courage will manifest itself in great leaders for, courageous leaders trust in the Lord more than they trust in man.**
>
> ➢ Our goal as great leaders is not to teach people to obey us, but they need to be taught to hear the Lord for themselves and respond to His will courageously.
>
> ➢ **Those who hear and obey courageous leadership will be among those who also become courageous. And Confusion Will No Longer Be An Issue.**

(Slides # 67 thru 70)
HANDLING IMPRISONMENT

Imprisonment allows time for the enemy to break down the spirit of people for the purpose of allowing them to voluntarily turn away from the Lord and render allegiance to worldly authorities.

> Though deep in their heart they may still believe in the Lord, some will give up. Ultimately, their life in this world will mean more to them than their faith in Christ.
>
> ➢ Satan rejoices when men will visibly turn away from Almighty God and render allegiance to him, even if it is not from a pure heart.
>
> ➢ Turning people to him is more important than murdering them, for it means he has defeated what is most important to God - the steadfast faithfulness of His people.
>
> ➢ **The one who has turned away from the Lord undoubtedly will be praised before the world as a newly enlightened hero. <u>This will be such a shameful experience</u>.**

Remain Steadfast During Times Of Persecution And Imprisonment.

> ➢ Although Christians may be physically overcome during this horrendous period of time; if they remain steadfast in their faith they are the ones who are victorious in this war.
>
> ➢ They have become outcasts from society, mocked at by former neighbors, family members, and friends, imprisoned and eventually, killed.
>
> ➢ This is the Body of Christ having a similar experience that their Lord Jesus Christ endured 2,000 years earlier.
>
> **They Are Now Glorious Participants In His Great Victory.**
> ➢ In the crucial test of faith, they have chosen to relinquish their lives rather than their faith in their God. <u>This is true victory.</u>

"Christian warriors, we are called to fight, not run from the battle."

<u>Notes:</u>

_____
_____
_____
_____
_____
_____
_____
_____

(Slides # 71 - 72)

TRUE CHRISTIANITY – A LIFE OF SELF-SACRIFICE

Soldiers in the army of God are committed to die to the world and live for the Lord Jesus Christ as the Son of Almighty God and the one and only way to eternal life.

If we die to this world, then there is nothing this world can do to us.

> ➢ For one who is dead to the world does not fear rejection or failure.

Being a soldier of the Cross is both the hardest and the easiest life we could live.

> ➢ It is hard because resisting our selfish, fleshly, prideful nature is very difficult.
>
> ➢ At the same time, it is easy - because living by the new nature of Christ - is the most wonderful life we could live.

THE LORD IS WORTHY OF THIS SELF-SACRIFICE DEVOTION
FOT HE ALSO SACRIFICED HIMSELF FOR US.

We may certainly suffer persecution from the worldly darkness, but when that happens, remember that God considers those who do suffer persecution as mightily worthy of His kingdom.

- ➢ When we lay down our lives, we truly find them. This is a comfort and peace far beyond what the world can give us.

- ➢ This doesn't mean we will be free of life problems, but as we fight the spiritual battle we are assured of victory.

- ➢ Therefore, we need to endure life's problems knowing that things will work out for the good.

When we are born-again, we are now behind enemy lines and the enemy is all around.

- ➢ **Christian warriors will never stick their heads in the sand.**

- ➢ **We are called to endure and continually encourage others - to also endure.**

Are you being called to a life of self-sacrifice? List how you want to move forward:

_____
_____
_____
_____
_____
_____
_____
_____
_____
_____
_____
_____
_____
_____
_____
_____
_____

BREAK-TIME   **(Slides # 73 - 74)**

(Slides # 75 - 76)

STEADFAST PRAYER WARRIORS WILL PREVAIL WITH GOD

Christian leaders need to remember that this is a Holy War and that the required power for victory is not found among its human participants, but in the power of God.

➢ Thus, believers need to understand the power of prayer which may be likened to that wrestling which took place between God and his chosen warriors throughout history.

➢ This is the "ongoing battle" that should be taking place within each member of the Body of Christ.

Key Points:

Believers must prevail with God before Satan can be subdued in their lives. Believers will never prevail by battling in the flesh.

➢ The victory is to be the Lord's and Christians can only prevail if they humble themselves before Him in true heart repentance. <u>Prayerlessness is proof that our life is still under the power of the flesh.</u> Prayerlessness is the cause of a powerless spiritual life.

➢ Victory is certain if believers will exercise the patient, long-suffering faith that brought His mighty warriors through the battlefield.

Remember, all of God's biblical warriors did lose some battles now and then, but they continued to be strengthened by their experiences and did not succumb to self-pity.

➢ That warrior spirit may be knocked down on occasion, but will always seek the strength of the Lord through prayer and fasting in order to get back up and again "run to the battle."

<u>These are the Christian warriors who will "never quit."</u>

Notes:

(Slides # 77 thru 79)

ANOINTED CHRISTIAN WARRIORS
PROCLAIMING THE FINAL GOSPEL OF THE KINGDOM

Christian warriors of the end-time generation will boldly and fearlessly stand united against the apostasy of this age as they proclaim the testimony of Jesus Christ and His truths among all the nations of the earth.

> ➤ *And this gospel of the kingdom will be proclaimed throughout the whole world as a testimony to all nations, and then the end will come. (**Matthew 24:14**)*

Key Points:

As to the contents of their message during a time of tribulation, these anointed witnesses for Christ will prayerfully stand before the Lord of the whole earth and they will speak nothing but that which their Lord has commissioned them to speak. That is:

They will speak of Christ and His atoning blood, which is the witness of the righteousness and holiness of God in the midst of a sinful world.

> ➤ *Jesus said to him, "I am the way, and the truth, and the life. No one comes to the Father except through me. (**John 14:6**)*
> ➤ *And there is salvation in no one else, for there is no other name under heaven given among men by which we must be saved." (**Acts 4:12**)*

They will openly condemn all efforts to seek salvation outside of that atoning blood.

> ➤ This will infuriate the false church and the worldly leadership that is attempting to establish a one-world kingdom together with a one-world religion.

> ➤ This will be a time of tremendous miracles as the gospel message goes forth in a power greater than the world has ever seen; a time when the blind will see, the deaf will hear, and many of the afflicted will be healed throughout the world.[54]

Notes:
_____
_____
_____
_____
_____

---

[54] John 14:12

(Slides # 80 thru 82)

A TIME OF GREAT HARVEST

This will be a time of great tribulation never before seen since the creation of the earth, <u>yet this also will be a time of a great harvest of souls.</u>

➢ A time of tremendous miracles as the gospel message goes forth in a power greater than the world has ever seen: the blind will see, the deaf will hear, and many of the afflicted will be healed throughout the world.

> *"Truly, truly, I say to you, whoever believes in me will also do the works that I do; and greater works than these will he do, because I am going to the Father. Whatever you ask in my name, this I will do, that the Father may be glorified in the Son. (**John 14:12-13**)*

Key Points:

The world must hear the gospel message proclaimed by His end-time warrior-spirited witnesses and they must hear it repeatedly so that they become fully conscious of their sin and the redemptive work of Jesus Christ:

1. All of mankind shall be well-acquainted with the gospel message of Jesus Christ before the final judgments fall on the earth.

2. There will be no more grey areas; one stands either with Christ or against Him - love and hatred will be clearly visible among all the inhabitants of the earth.

3. Those who reject Him will do so willingly and deliberately - then the testimony is finished and may be silenced.

4. Those who scorn the message will be without excuse when they stand before the judgment seat of almighty God.

5. Certainly many people will respond and be brought into everlasting life, but the great majority of the world will blasphemy this message and will persecute those who proclaim it.

Finally, this gospel message not only will be a calling to mankind to repent and give glory to God, but it also will contain the prophetic warning that final judgments are soon coming to the world.

Notes:
_____
_____
_____
_____
_____
_____

(Slides # 83 thru 85)

WALKING AS GOD'S WARRIORS DAY TO DAY

Redeeming the Time

- This may be extremely difficult, but it is also one of the most important areas of daily life that champion leaders must master.

- Stay on the offensive; take the sword of the Spirit, which is the Word of God, and know it, memorize it, and take it up daily.

- Stand firm; when under daily fire, remember Job. Intercessory prayer must become heart driven, for this is where your one-on-one relationship with the Lord truly grows powerful.

Fasting, together with Prayer,

- **Fasting** is a very critical area for those who are called to warrior leadership in the coming days.

- We need to embrace our biblical calling to **"fast"** for this is a great channel for spiritual power.

- Important insights into understanding our call to biblical fasting are available in a **handout**.

A Time of Great Opportunity:

- For those who hear this call to be warriors and overcomers, this is an opportunity that was offered to warriors like Paul, David, and Elijah, and it is offered to each of us in our lives.

- We only have one life and thus, one opportunity to stand for our Lord on the front lines of the battlefield and fight against His enemies.

- The rewards that are promised in the afterlife are predicated upon our kingdom work during this lifetime.

- Some will rule ten cities, some five, and some one, but most will be citizens, not leaders. All will receive rewards, but there is a difference—His warriors will be called to eternal leadership in the eternal kingdom.

- **Let your faith shine within your environment; remove the basket, and be the glorious light that you are called to be in the world.**

Let us not go to the grave wishing that we had answered this call. Now is the time, not tomorrow or next week; the call is now to "those who hear."

(Slides # 86 - 87)
THE ARMY OF GOD IS FOR "VOLUNTEERS ONLY:"

The common purpose for all volunteers in the Army of God is to prepare in the bootcamp of our prayer closets in order to allow the light and glory of our Commander-in-Chief, Jesus Christ to be clearly manifested on the spiritual battlefield which lies in the midst of this world.

- ➢ Our Commander-in-Chief does not draft His soldiers, but He opens His arms and welcomes all those who volunteer. He does not employ emotional strategies, but simply speaks out of love and calls each of us to join Him on the battlefield.

- ➢ Although he calls us to join Him in His battle against the forces of evil, He leaves us free to join the enemy against Him if we so will. He makes no promises that we will become rich or not experience pain in this life.

- ➢ Christian warriors who will stand fast in teaching others and will not compromise the true gospel are His disciples whom He values deeply.

<u>Our Choice – Will We or Won't We?</u>
- ➢ **We are faced with the option of greatness as a leader in the Kingdom of God, but we can choose to settle for less. If we decide for greatness, it will cost us everything we have and are. WE WILL HAVE TO SURRENDER OUR LIFE.**

- ➢ **The Choice Is Momentous, But Amazingly, It Is Ours To Make.**

(Slides # 88 thru 92)
COMRADESHIP – STRENGTHENS THE ARMY OF GOD

This is very important to Jesus as He speaks to His Father:

> "I do not ask for these only, but also for those who will believe in me through their word, **that they may all be one**, just as you, Father, are in me, and I in you, that they also may be in us, so that the world may believe that you have sent me. *John 17:20-21*

Being in the Lord's army is much more than just fighting battles. It also is about uniting in community with Him to be built into a spiritual family that will spend eternity together.

- ➢ Comradeship in combat is one of the deepest and unique bonds one can experience.

- ➢ Those who go though the fire together develop a unique heart bonding with one another.
- ➢ This strong fellowship is also meant to be among those in the army of God a bonding so close that those who are part of it cannot be separated.

- ➢ This was certainly the characteristic of those who strongly supported David and became known as "mighty men of Israel." They could not be defeated.

Also, the Lord's small group of disciples, who obeyed His commands,
- ➢ **CHANGED THE WORLD MORE THAN ANY WORLDLY CONQUEROR.**

A Very Powerful Bonding Among His Soldiers Was Extremely Important To Jesus.

> Again I say to you, if two of you agree on earth about anything they ask, it will be done for them by my Father in heaven. **For where two or three are gathered in my name, there am I among them."** *Matthew 18:19-20*

To Bond Together At The Depth That The Lord Is Seeking -----
We Must Start With A Small Group

Marine units in the military also use this principle.

➤ These units are built on 4-man fire-teams. Three of these teams make up a squad and three squads make up a platoon, and then it grows through the organization of companies, battalions, regiments, and divisions.

➤ Yet the basic foundational units of the Corps are these four-man fire-teams.

➤ **In a combat firefight, these fire-teams are more committed to each other than the larger unit. They have bonded together in like-mindedness.**

Jesus' Greatest Works And Deepest Teachings Were Given To Small Groups.

➤ He did not walk on the water in front of everyone. Could it be that the Lord prefers doing His greatest miracles with the fewest witnesses.

➤ The Lord had a ministry to the multitudes but He gave far more attention to His closest disciples.

➤ With the 12 He went much deeper and invested more time. Then with the three (Peter, James, & John), He shared everything.

➤ Balanced ministries need to have relationships on all three levels --- the multitudes --- those who follow & support the ministry --- the closest of one's friends.

These small groups should meet together frequently and begin by praying for spiritual strength found in Ephesians 3:14-21

Notes:

_____
_____
_____
_____
_____
_____
_____

(Slides # 93 - 94)

LEADERSHIP PRIORITIES IN THE KINGDOM OF GOD

> **Remember these Priorities every Single Day:**
>
> ➢ 1st – We fight for the glory of His wondrous Name in the midst of a world of darkness.
>
> ➢ 2nd – We fight for the salvation of those in bondage to the enemy. Family, friends, co-workers and strangers that our Lord brings into our lives.
>
> ➢ 3rd – We fight without fear for ourselves for we are called to let go of this life and not be concerned for the consequences that may befall us.

Finally, my dear brothers and sisters who are hearing this message – may our Lord powerfully anoint you to be mighty warrior-spirited witnesses for the Lord Jesus Christ and the Kingdom of God as you travel though the wilderness of this life

> ➢ *Arise, shine, for your light has come, and the glory of the Lord has risen upon you. For behold, darkness shall cover the earth, and thick darkness the peoples; but the Lord will arise upon you, and his glory will be seen upon you.* (**Isaiah 60:1-2**)

PRAYER FOR SPIRITUAL STRENGTH

Ephesians 3:14-21

> *For this reason I bow my knees before the Father, from whom every family in heaven and on earth is named, that according to the riches of his glory he may grant you to be strengthened with power through his Spirit in your inner being, so that Christ may dwell in your hearts through faith—that you, being rooted and grounded in love, may have strength to comprehend with all the saints what is the breadth and length and height and depth, and to know the love of Christ that surpasses knowledge, that you may be filled with all the fullness of God. Now to him who is able to do far more abundantly than all that we ask or think, according to the power at work within us, to him be glory in the church and in Christ Jesus throughout all generations, forever and ever. Amen.*

THE LAMB OF GOD - OUR TRUE "COMMANDER-IN-CHIEF"

The days are rapidly approaching when a tremendous separation will take place among mankind.

Yet, during this present era of warfare, He reigns as our Commander-in-Chief and His Name continues to be the battle cry for those warriors who fight daily for righteousness and truth.

His name is Jesus, Our Lord, Our King, Our Commander-in-Chief

➢ A truly mighty Leader who would never delegate assignments to His people that He Himself wouldn't readily embrace.

➢ A Commander that Christian warriors will readily follow not matter the danger or what costs have to be paid.

➢ These are warriors whose deepest desire is to hear Jesus welcome them with the following words when they enter into His presence:

> .... 'Well done, good and faithful servant. You have been faithful over a little; I will set you over much. Enter into the joy of your master.' *Matthew 25:21*

MINISTRY and RESOURCES

To arrange for speaking engagements with Dr. Don Bell use the following contact information:
- Email: Dr.Don.Bell@mcgmin.com
- Review Dr. Bell's profile at: www.mcgmin.com/authors.html
- Call: (888) 575-9626

This workbook, Keep What is Written, follows Dr. Bell's lesson series available on www.equippingwatchmen.com. This important lesson series is based on the following book:

God's Anointed Warriors
By Dr. Donald Bell (available now.)

This book brings 21st century clarity to prophetic events recorded in the book of Revelation and the Lord's calling for warrior-spirited Christians of this generation.

We are right on the verge of devastating events that will create great fear and chaos throughout the world and especially in our increasingly immoral and comfort-seeking nation.

The reader is encouraged to follow Dr. Donald Bell in his in-depth study of Scripture that will bring greater clarity to numerous end-time events recorded in the Book of Revelation -events which are currently unfolding before our very eyes.

ISBN 978-1-943412-08-2

Published by -
Wilderness Voice Publishing
Canon City, Colorado USA
www.wvpbooks.com

This valuable resource can be obtained by the following:
- Amazon.com - Search: God's Anointed Warriors By Dr. Donald Bell
- Order from your local bookstore: ISBN 978-1-943412-08-2
- Wilderness Voice Publishing: https://www.mcgmin.com